THE ROCK SNOB*S DICTIONARY

THE ROCK SNOB*S DICTIONARY

AN ESSENTIAL LEXICON OF ROCKOLOGICAL KNOWLEDGE

*Rock Snob *n* reference term for
the sort of pop connoisseur for whom
the actual enjoyment of music is but a side dish
to the accumulation of arcane knowledge

David Kamp & Steven Daly

Illustrated by Ross MacDonald

Sanctuary

Printed in the United Kingdom by MPG Books, Bodmin

Published by Sanctuary Publishing Limited, Sanctuary House, 45-53 Sinclair Road, London W14 0NS, United Kingdom

www.sanctuarypublishing.com

First edition published 2005

The Rock Snob*s Dictionary is based on material originally published in *Vanity Fair*.

Book design by Ellen Cipriano

Cover Design by Tara O'Leary

ISBN 1-86074-651-9

Contents

Acknowledgments

The authors wish to thank their wives; their families; Graydon Carter; Dana Brown; Charles Conrad; Beth Haymaker; Alison Presley; Suzanne Gluck; Erin Malone; Bob Mack; Richard Metzger; David Gates; Listen Records of Glasgow, Scotland; and Jim Babjak's Flamin' Groovies of New Brunswick, New Jersey. As well as all the truculent store clerks who have peevishly waited upon us.

An Introductory Note by the Authors

The Rock Snob is a confounding person in your life. On one hand, he brooks no ignorance of pop-music history and will take violent umbrage at the fact that you've never heard of the noted rock arranger and soundtrack composer Jack Nitzsche, much less heard Nitzsche's ambitious pop-classical album, *St. Giles Cripplegate*. On the other hand, he will not countenance the notion that you know more than he about a certain area of music. If, for example, you mention that *Fun House* is your favorite Stooges album, he will respond that it "lacks the visceral punch of 'I Wanna Be Your Dog' from a year earlier, but it's got some superb howling from Iggy and coruscating riffage from Ron Asheton, though not on the level of James Williamson's on *Raw Power*"—this indigestible clump of words acting as a cudgel with which the Rock Snob is trumping you and marking the turf as his.

*The Rock Snob*s Dictionary* was conceived, in part, to enable non-Snobs to hold their own in such distressing situations, with the added benefit of sparing them the trouble of actually listening to the music in question. However, the dictionary is equally useful as a primer for curious music fans who sincerely want to learn more about rock but are intimidated by unexplained, ultra-knowing references in the music press to "Stax-y horns," "chiming, plangent

Rickenbackers," and "Eno." The authors have painstakingly catalogued the fundaments of Rock Snobbery—e.g., *Who is Nick Drake? Why should I care about the deceased rock critic Lester Bangs? What is this "Hammond B3" thing that they keep talking about?*—and distilled years of arduous research into concise, alphabetized knowledge pellets. The dictionary's compactness and portability make it an ideal on-site crisis-resolution tool in independent record shops where the supercilious clerks won't deign to explain, say, the difference between the Soft Boys and the Soft Machine. Much as overwhelmed oenophiles-in-training tote Robert Parker's pocket wine guide to their local vintner's for guidance, so may the Snob-in-training consult *The Rock Snob*'s Dictionary* as he peruses the racks and weighs whether to purchase Van Dyke Parks's *Song Cycle* or Dr. John's *Gris-Gris*. And though most of the Snob canon consists of music that's actually quite listenable, the authors have not shied away from sounding a word of warning about the follies of certain revisionist Snobs, who, in their eagerness to claim a "discovery," recklessly elevate the reputation of such flagrantly second-rate acts as Badfinger and Delaney & Bonnie. In addition, the authors have included helpful sidebars, such as the Guide to Snob Nomenclature (the Velvet Underground's drummer is to be referred to as Mo, *never* Maureen, Tucker), to further advance readers' Snob educations and to avert embarrassing faux pas in the cocktail-party bull sessions that inevitably transpire near the host's stereo.

The authors caution readers that *The Rock Snob*'s Dictionary* is not meant to serve as a comprehensive rock-music reference in the vein of *The Rolling Stone Encyclopedia of Rock & Roll*. Just because a musician has enjoyed lasting success and critical acclaim doesn't mean he warrants inclusion here. *Only the persons and entities that are the psychic property of Rock Snobs make the cut.* For example, there is no entry for David Crosby, because practically every person over thirty knows who he is and can hum a few bars of "Teach Your Children." However, the late Gene Clark, Crosby's colleague in the original lineup of the Byrds, warrants an entry because, while the average Joe hasn't the faintest idea who he is, the Rock Snob has fetishized him for his poor-selling post-Byrds output of country rock and orchestral pop. Occasionally, there will be an entry that seems to buck this policy, that will seem familiar to lay readers—such as Dion, ubiquitous on oldies radio via "The Wanderer" and "A Teenager in Love," or Dexys Midnight Runners, the eighties British pop group of "Come On Eileen" repute—but appearances are deceptive. These artists warrant inclusion in *The Rock Snob*s Dictionary* because Snobs value them for utterly different reasons than non-Snobs do—in Dion's case, for his post-drug-rehab forays into folk music and MOR pop in the late sixties and early seventies; in Dexys Midnight Runners' case, for the alienating, absurdist post-"Eileen" work of the group's key member, Kevin Rowland. For all intents and purposes, there are two Dions and two Dexyses, the Snob and non-Snob versions. The latter versions, being accessible and commercially successful and all, don't warrant our consideration here.

A Brief History of Rock Snobbery

Since the dawn of rock, there have been individuals, usually young men of argumentative tendencies, who have lorded their encyclopedic musical knowledge over others.

In the movie *Diner*, the filmmaker Barry Levinson adroitly depicts an early specimen of this type with the character Shrevie, played by Daniel Stern, who dresses down his wife for misfiling one of his 45s, and, in the same fit of pique, boasts of knowing the producer, year, label, and B-side title of every single he owns. By the seventies, the legions of such pedants had grown considerably thanks to the emergence of a credible rock press. Via *Rolling Stone* and *Creem* in America and *Melody Maker* and the *New Musical Express* in Britain, one could easily track the latest developments in Captain Beefheart's career and vicariously experience David Bowie's gigs with the Spiders from Mars, even if one was underage or wary of actually commingling with sweaty, hirsute rock people in the flesh.

But it wasn't until the eighties that Rock Snobbery truly gained traction as a phenomenon and pathology. This was attributable chiefly to two developments: the advent of the "classic rock" radio format, which saw rock aficionados retreat from their monomaniacal obsession with the new, and the rise of the CD format, which A) compelled fans to repurchase their entire music collections, and B) compelled the record labels to reissue their back catalogues with "bonus tracks" and booklets featuring never-before-seen photographs and exhaustive liner notes. Rock knowledge, even of the most arcane sort, was suddenly common currency and a salable commodity, valuable and significant beyond one's immediate circle of loser friends. Independent labels such as Rhino and Sundazed astutely took advantage of this situation, broadening the Snob mandate beyond the mere revisiting of one's old favorites and trawling the archives for out-of-print records that could be digitalized, remastered, and packaged as "lost masterpieces" and "forgotten gems." The attendant press coverage created a new roster of Snob heroes whose underappreciatedness was, in the Snob purview, a societal crime: Gram Parsons, Curt Boettcher, Fred Neil, Alex Chilton, Shuggie Otis. Which is not to say that the Rock Snob was some hidebound, patchouli-drenched anachronism who lived strictly in the past—he was, by definition, *in touch*, and thus, his fear of calcification ensured that he kept up with developments in hip-hop and electronica as surely as he collected Syd Barrett bootlegs.

By the dawn of the twenty-first century, Rock Snobbery had become so widespread that some old-line Snobs felt under siege, their carefully hoarded knowledge of Harry Smith's *Anthology of American Folk Music* no longer special in the wake of the *O Brother, Where Art Thou?* roots-music explosion, their rare mint vinyl copies of Shuggie Otis's *Inspiration Information* rendered worthless by the album's loving reissue on CD—an indignity exacerbated by the title track's inclusion on a Starbucks compilation. But the fact is, Rock Snobbery, far from having been undermined, had reached epidemic proportions. While the fogy stereotype still occasionally rang true—the Snob as embodied by Nick Hornby's aging hipster protagonist in *High Fidelity* or by the indignant boomer who writes to *Mojo* magazine complaining that Radiohead is too young to appear on the cover—the Rock Snob phenomenon had grown to encompass both sexes and all ages: The twenty-something Jack White covered Dusty Springfield tunes and took it upon himself to produce Loretta Lynn's comeback album; the teen heroine of Disney's 2003 remake of *Freaky Friday* affectionately cradled "my dad's Strat"; and such Snob lodestars as the Pixies, the Stooges, and the New York Dolls exhumed themselves for sold-out reunion shows that were attended not only by nostalgic graybeards but by kids who missed out on these bands the first time around.

The Snob fraternity has also benefited from the very public advocacy of its celebrity membership, a roster whose number includes such musicians as Morrissey, Beck, Elvis Costello, and the Beastie Boys and such music-savvy film directors as Wes Anderson, Martin Scorsese, and Cameron Crowe. These individuals, all of unimpeachably exquisite musical taste, play a sort of curatorial role for the masses, using their platforms to familiarize civilians with such Snobworthies as Jobriath, Serge Gainsbourg, David Ackles, Lee "Scratch" Perry, Nico, and Harry Nilsson. In some cases this role has been formalized, with the Luminary Snob actually mandated by an institution to propagate his Snobbery. Both Costello and the producer Hal Willner have served stints in UCLA's Artist-in-Residence program, where they have been charged by the university with organizing conceptual concert series; Willner really pulled out all the stops with his two-day Harry Smith tribute in 2001, which featured Costello, Beck, Bill Frisell, Todd Rundgren, Marianne Faithfull, and Richard Thompson, among others. And, since 1993, London's Royal Festival Hall has hosted a summertime concert series called Meltdown in which a guest Snob curator—past overseers include Morrissey, Laurie Anderson, Nick Cave, Scott Walker, and, inevitably, Costello—rounds up his favorite "seminal" acts for a de facto Snob Woodstock.

Though non-Snobs still far outnumber Snobs in the general population, the demographics of Snobbery are skewing ever younger. Taken in tandem with the aforementioned advances in Snob education, this trend augurs further gains in the Snob population and a future in which even preschoolers will be able to differentiate between the

Louvin Brothers and the Stanley Brothers. Such being the case, the authors promise to be diligent in tracking new Snob trends for subsequent editions of this book.

Helpful Hints

Given the complexities and interconnections of the Snob universe, cross-references between entries are common and are spelled out in CAPITAL LETTERS for easy identification. The authors have also seen fit to identify certain entries with the Rock Snob Vanguard icon , the presence of which indicates an entry subject who is held in especially sacred regard by Rock Snobs, e.g., the Rickenbacker guitar and the combustibly short-lived baroque-pop band Love.

Finally, let us express our sincere hope that this reference performs a valuable public service, acting not only to edify musically inquisitive readers, but to bridge cultural gaps between Snobs and non-Snobs, many of whom sleep under the same roof but live lives fraught with unnecessary vintage-vinyl-related tension.

Oh, and by the way, the cool Beatles song for Snobs to like is "Cry Baby Cry," off side 4 of the *White Album*.

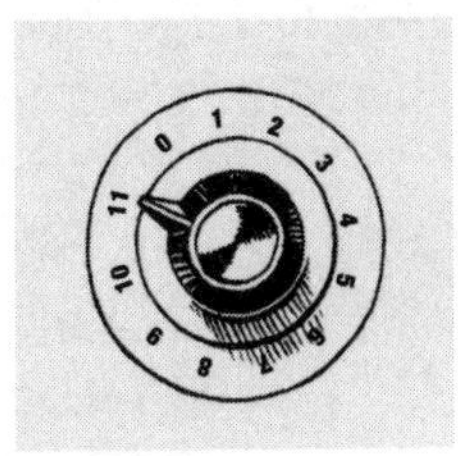

THE ROCK SNOB*S DICTIONARY

The Rock Snob*s Dictionary

A ⊛ symbol indicates a Rock Snob Vanguard item, denoting a person or an entity held in particular esteem by Rock Snobs.

Acetate. A small-batch test-pressing of a recording, used for demonstration purposes in the pre-digital era—so that record-label executives could vet an upcoming release, or so that music publishers could pitch their new songs to the labels. Often used synonymously with the term WHITE LABEL, though a true, vintage acetate, recorded straight from the studio master tapes and cut on heavy, fragile lacquer that wore out after a few plays (as opposed to the more durable vinyl), is an even rarer commodity. *The official Brunswick release of "My Generation" kicks ass, but it doesn't quite capture the primal mod savagery of the* acetate.

Ackles, David. Hard-luck Californian singer-songwriter who released four cultishly worshipped albums from 1968 to 1974, the most celebrated of which is *American Gothic* (1972). Like his poor-selling contemporaries VAN DYKE PARKS and Randy Newman, Ackles, in his work, evoked the great American songbooks of Stephen Foster and George and Ira Gershwin more than he did the stoner confessionals of the LAUREL CANYON troupe, making him something of a man out of time—though he would later be praised as a genius by Elvis Costello and Bernie Taupin, Elton John's lyricist. Ackles died of cancer in 1999, before a proposed collaboration with Taupin could be realized.

Adler, Lou. Malibu-based *macher* of the L.A. music scene since the late fifties, having discovered Jan & Dean, shepherded JOHN PHILLIPS and the Mamas and the Papas to stardom on his Dunhill label, organized the MONTEREY POP festival, cofounded the Sunset Strip clubs the Whisky a Go-Go and the Roxy, and produced Carole King's denimy singer-songwriter showpiece, *Tapestry,* in 1971, thereby bringing the LAUREL CANYON ethos to the mass market. A cool, inscrutable figure who often sits beside Jack Nicholson at Lakers games, Adler functions as the urbane antithesis to the scrappy guttersnipe Strip scenesters KIM FOWLEY and RODNEY BINGENHEIMER.

Albini, Steve. Self-consciously difficult Chicago-based record producer who chafes at being called a producer, insisting that he merely "records" bands; best known for having produced—er, recorded—Nirvana's studio swan song, *In Utero*, and for issuing snarky comments to the press when some of the album's uncompromisingly raw songs were later remixed by other producers. Albini, who pushes the bounds of hard-rock iconoclasm by *wearing glasses and having short hair*, enhanced his outsider cred by playing guitar in the not-very-good hardcore

Steve Albini

bands Big Black, Rapeman, and Shellac. *Man, that drum sound is a monster! No one knows mic placement like* Albini.

Alt.country. Self-righteous rock-country hybrid genre whose practitioners favor warbly, studiedly imperfect vocals, nubby flannel shirts, and a conviction that their take on country is more "real" than the stuff coming out of Nashville. Heavily influenced by GRAM PARSONS. Also known as the No Depression movement, after the title of an album by the SEMINAL alt.country band Uncle Tupelo (which itself purloined the title from the CARTER FAMILY song "No Depression in Heaven"). Though such alt.country standard-bearers as the Jayhawks and Neko Case continue to embrace the genre's conventions, the former Uncle Tupelo mainmen Jeff Tweedy and Jay Farrar have emphatically de-twangified, the former as the leader of the crit-beloved pop eclecticists Wilco, the latter as a solo artist after disbanding his post-Tupelo alt.country band, Son Volt.

Americana. Catchall term for any indigenous American music that draws influence from the United States' earthier pre-rock idioms (country, folk, bluegrass, etc.) and bears no obvious imprimatur of slick New York and Los Angeles A&R men; used to describe everything from mail-order-only cassettes sold by West Virginia fiddlers to high-profile ALT.COUNTRY releases by attractive, slightly wind-chapped young women such as Tift Merritt and Laura Cantrell.

Anthology of American Folk Music, The. Multivolume collection, first issued by the FOLKWAYS label in 1952, of obscure and semi-obscure folk recordings as compiled by eccentric musicologist Harry Smith (1923–1991). Significant for having allegedly triggered the late-fifties–early-sixties "folkie" movement that gave us Bob Dylan, and therefore, by extension, for making pop music subversive, turning the Beatles into druggies, and irreparably rending the fabric of our society.

Anti-folk. Hazily defined genre originally inhabited by young white tenement squatters who combined folk and punk sensibilities, but more recently embodied by the LO-FI pretend rustics Will Oldham and Bill Callahan, who, under their aliases (Palace and Bonnie "Prince" Billy for Oldham, Smog for Callahan), thrum acoustic guitars and warble ominous murder-ballad lyrics in the style of the authentic twenties hayseeds heard on Harry Smith's *ANTHOLOGY OF AMERICAN FOLK MUSIC.* The anti-folk movement (which took its name from English acousti-punk Billy Bragg's description of his own sound) traces its origins to a scroungy eighties Lower East Side scene that spawned, among others, Beck, Michelle Shocked, Cindy Lee Berryhill, and Ani DiFranco.

Aphrodite's Child. Hirsute, preposterous Greek PROG outfit from the late sixties and early seventies enjoying new life as a staple of retro-funk compilations. After the group's 1972 split, walrus-sized vocalist Demis Roussos, possessor of an unlikely castrato singing voice, went on to dubious Euro-fame as a kind of Hellenic Barry White, crooning MOR love songs for the après-ski set, while keyboardist Vangelis Parpathanssiou jettisoned his last name and won international fame for his synth-heroic soundtrack to *Chariots of Fire* and Snob plaudits for his noirish *Blade Runner* soundtrack.

Arden, Don. Knuckle-dragging thug-titan of Britain's early rock scene; the Suge Knight of his era. Gaining a toe-hold in London's postwar show business scene as a boy comedian and singer, Arden (né Harold Levy) muscled his way into promotion, organizing British tours for such kindred-spirit wildmen as Gene Vincent, Little Richard, and Jerry Lee Lewis. As manager of THE SMALL FACES, Black Sabbath, and the Electric Light Orchestra in the sixties and seventies, Arden earned a singular reputation for violence, famously dangling fellow maverick Robert Stigwood from a balcony during a business dispute. When Arden's daughter Sharon took over the management of his client Ozzy Osbourne in the early eighties, marrying the cro-mag rocker in the process, Don declared war on Sharon, and she tried to run him over with a car. But Arden has mellowed in recent years, reconciling with his daughter and shuffling through episodes of MTV's *The Osbournes* while singing Yiddish music-hall songs.

Don Arden

Association, the. Prime arbiters of the late-sixties "sunshine pop" ethos, having scored a string of featherlight CURT BOETTCHER–produced hits such as "Along Comes Mary," "Cherish," and "Windy." Though the Association was big enough to have been the opening act at the MONTEREY POP festival, and their multilayered harmonies and sophisticated arrangements were sometimes worthy of BRIAN WILSON, their credibility was hampered by their wussy image, relentless deployment of *ba-pa-ba-paaah* backing vocals, and the fact that their main musical force, Terry Kirkman, played the recorder and flute onstage—ultimately consigning them, perhaps unfairly, to the BUBBLEGUM ranks.

Austin City Limits. Public-television program originally conceived, in 1974, as a showcase for Austin, Texas's burgeoning music scene—the first guest was the pre-superstardom Willie Nelson—but later reconfigured as a hip, wide-ranging TV alternative to Nashville's fogyish Grand Ole Opry (with such guests as TOWNES VAN ZANDT, Emmylou Harris, Rosanne Cash, and Lyle Lovett), and, later still, as a magical melting-pot for both mainstream country acts (Alan Jackson, Brooks & Dunn, Vince Gill), and ROOTS-sensitive rock and pop acts like Sheryl Crow, the Jayhawks, and Ben Kweller. *Rodney Crowell turned in a smokin' set on* Austin City Limits *last night.*

Autoharp. Small stringed instrument, also known as a chorded zither, whose gentle twang, portability, and visual appeal (it's cradled in one arm and stroked by the other, like a newborn) have made it a favorite of both old-timey musicians (such as the CARTER FAMILY) and newfangled AMERICANA artists. Catherine O'Hara strummed one in the folkie send-up *A Mighty Wind.*

Axe. Imbecilic term for an electric guitar, nevertheless embraced by rock critics and hobby guitarists with advanced degrees. *My Sebring* axe *doesn't have the pedigree of a Fender, but man, it can shred like one!*

Axelrod, David. Snob-exhumed purveyor of sixties orchestral funk. A West Coast producer-arranger with a CV worthy of a James Ellroy character—as a young man he dabbled in violent crime and went on to become a jazz producer in the fifties—Axelrod established himself in the mid-sixties producing artists as varied as Lou Rawls and the Electric Prunes, and under his own name recorded ambitious, layered albums that defied categorization. (He once used Blake poems as lyrics.) A commercial failure in his own era, Axelrod embarked on a cocaine-fueled downward spiral, but fortune smiled upon him in the nineties when the likes of Lauryn Hill, Dr. Dre, and DJ Shadow sampled his work.

Bacharach, Burt. Rehabilitated songwriter whose metrically and melodically unorthodox sixties pop-luxe hits, such as "Anyone Who Had a Heart" and "I Say a Little Prayer" (written with lyricist Hal David), were dismissed for two decades as square and Muzaky until Rock Snobs decided in the nineties that it was okay to like them again. Particularly active latter-day boosters have been Noel Gallagher of Oasis and Elvis Costello, with whom Bacharach recorded a 1998 "comeback" album. *That song has a very* Bacharach*esque flügelhorn part.*

Burt Bacharach

Bad Brains. Hard-luck jazz-fusion weirdos from Washington, D.C., who cashed in on the New York hardcore punk scene in 1980 with their minute-and-a-half-long single "Pay to Cum." The subsequent introduction of reggae and heavy-metal elements into Bad Brains' sound did little for their sales but everything for their legend, as evidenced by the band's feverish championing by the Rock Snob collective the Beastie Boys.

Badfinger. Ill-starred POWER-POP quartet signed to the Beatles' Apple Records under the aegis of mentor Paul McCartney, who saw them as the heirs to his rupturing group—a patently flawed premise nevertheless embraced today by Revisionist Snobs. Led by shag-haired songwriters Pete Ham and Tom Evans, Badfinger achieved early success with a string of melodic ballads (such as the McCartney-penned "Come and Get It" and their own "Day After Day") and saw a HARRY NILSSON cover of their song "Without You" go all the way to No. 1 on the U.S. charts. But they couldn't sustain the high quality of their early material and fell apart, riven by internal strife and legal wrangles. A despairing Ham committed suicide in 1975, and Evans followed suit in 1983.

Bambaataa, Afrika. Zulu-centric OLD-SCHOOL Bronx DJ whose 1982 hit "Planet Rock" put Tommy Boy Records on the map and fused hip-hop with Caucasoid electronic music, built as it was around a figure from KRAFTWERK's "Trans-Europe Express." Despite his gang-member past and imposing cyborg mien (winged shades, hooded robes, VOCODER-ized vocals), Bambaataa proved an affable ambassador of hip-hop culture to the white world, performing at such Downtown new-wave clubs as the Mudd Club and the Peppermint Lounge in the early eighties while presiding over his own "Zulu Nation" collective of DJs and b-boys Uptown.

Bangs, Lester. Dead rock critic canonized for his willfully obnoxious, amphetamine-streaked prose. Writing chiefly for *Creem* magazine, Bangs stuck two fingers down the throat of the counterculture elite and kept alive the scuzzy legacy of bands such as the Velvet Underground, THE STOOGES, and the MC5. Though every Rock Snob worth his salt reveres Bangs (a heavy biography by Rock Snob author Jim DeRogatis was published a few years ago), his writing has aged rather less well than that of his less strident contemporaries Richard Meltzer and Nick Tosches. *They're all pussies at* Rolling Stone *now, man; not a* Lester Bangs *among them.*

Barrett, Syd. Founding member of Pink Floyd who defined the group's early sound with his juvenile, peculiarly English take on psychedelia. Already in the process of becoming rock's most celebrated acid casualty at the time of Pink Floyd's 1967 debut, Barrett left the band in 1968, managing to record two solo albums of skeletal meanderings (one of them entitled *The Madcap Laughs*) before drifting into the permanent twilight in which he lives today. The post-Barrett Floyd song "Shine On You Crazy Diamond" is about him.

Baxter, Jeff "Skunk." Gregarious, droopily mustached veteran guitarist, formerly of Steely Dan and the Doobie Brothers. Long regarded as the session pro's session pro, Baxter has recently forfeited his consummate-insider status by becoming ubiquitous as a commentator in VH1 and BBC rockumentaries. He also enjoys an implausible side career as an adviser to Congress and the Pentagon on ballistic-missile defense.

Beefheart, Captain. Performing name of Don Van Vliet, a California-desert kid and childhood friend of Frank Zappa's whose 1969 album, *Trout Mask Replica*, is, Rock Snobs swear, a classic whose brilliance will reveal itself after you've listened to it 6,000 times or so. A typical

Beefheart song showcased Van Vliet yawping dementedly over the intricately arranged yet chaotic-sounding playing of his backing group, the Magic Band, whose members used "wacky" stage names such as Zoot Horn Rollo and Antennae Jimmy Semens.

Captain Beefheart

Van Vliet retired from music in the early eighties and is now a painter. *His aesthetic may be straight out of the Dust Bowl, but Tom Waits's strangulated vocals have a soupçon of* Beefheart *about them.*

Big Star. Anglophilic early-seventies American combo whose first two albums, *#1 Record* and *Radio City*, have Koran-like status in POWER-POP circles. Led by Memphis native Alex Chilton, who began his career as a teenager with the blue-eyed-soul boys the Box Tops ("The Letter"), Big Star recorded tunes that, while catchy, were too fraught with druggy tension to be commercial—thereby guaranteeing the group posthumous "great overlooked band" status. Chilton, who later had a REPLACEMENTS song named after him, is now a rheumy-eyed eccentric who occasionally performs with original Big Star drummer Jody Stephens and their adoring acolytes at quasi-reunion shows.

Bingenheimer, Rodney. Gnomish L.A. scenester and dogged Anglophile who washed up on the Sunset Strip in the mid-sixties as a teen, attached himself to every musician passing through, and parlayed his shameless parasitism into a pop career, an improbably active sex life, and infamy as "The Mayor of Sunset Strip" (a title bestowed upon him by the actor Sal Mineo and later used as the name of a bathetic rockumentary about him). Though long known to Angelenos as a POWER-POP-mad DJ on KROQ (where he is now relegated to the Sunday-night graveyard shift), Bingenheimer enjoyed his poptastic apogee as the proprietor-namesake of Rodney Bingenheimer's English Disco, a short-lived but bustling club that was the locus of the American GLAM scene in the early seventies.

Black Flag. SEMINAL California hardcore punk band, occasionally confused by novice Snobs with STEVE ALBINI's Big Black. At the time of its 1978 recording debut on its own SST label, Black Flag had a revolving-vocalist policy, but that changed in 1981 when the job was handed permanently to square-jawed, stage-invading fan Henry Rollins. After the band split in 1986, founding Black Flag bassist Greg Ginn devoted his energies to SST, which released the early albums of proto-grunge bands Hüsker Dü, SONIC YOUTH, and Dinosaur Jr., as well as those of his own band, Gone; Rollins cut his hair and strenuously cultivated an image as a Renaissance man, starting his own publishing company (named 2.13.61, after his birthdate), releasing solo albums, moonlighting as an actor, and winning a Grammy in 1994 for a "spoken word" album.

Blow, Kurtis. Kangol-hatted, Jheri-curled hip-hop pioneer whose 1980 hit "The Breaks" was the first rap single to go gold. Though his disco-tinged material holds up less well than the more muscular work of fellow pioneers Melle Mel and AFRIKA BAMBAATAA, Blow has astutely positioned himself as hip-hop's curator of all things OLD SCHOOL, hosting an early-rap show on Sirius satel-

Kurtis Blow

lite radio, plotting a documentary about hip-hop's origins, and contributing liner notes and his good name to RHINO RECORDS's *Kurtis Blow Presents: The History of Rap* series.

Blue Cheer. Hirsute, unsightly San Francisco power trio of sludgy ineptitude, affectionately remembered as the loudest-ever rock band; Snob lore has it that the sheer volume of the noise coming out of guitarist Leigh Stephens's amps caused a dog to seize up and die at one of their concerts. While the band's 1968 debut *Vincebus Eruptum* set new standards for lumpen blues-rock brutality and was arguably the first heavy-metal album, Blue Cheer soon succumbed to a series of *Spinal Tap*–esque lineup changes and fell into obscurity, never repeating the Top 40 success of its 1968 desecration of Eddie Cochran's "Summertime Blues." *For sheer, colonoscopizing sonic assault, nobody, not even Hendrix or the Who, could touch* Blue Cheer.

Boettcher, Curt. Impossibly saccharine singer, songwriter, and producer of devoutly lightweight West Coast "sunshine pop" in the sixties, and therefore the lodestar of the 1990s EASY-LISTENING revival. A rare gay figure in the relentlessly skirt-chasing L.A.-pop milieu, Boettcher achieved his greatest commercial success as the producer of THE ASSOCIATION's mid-sixties hits "Along Comes Mary" and "Cherish." His recordings released under his own name, and with the groups the Ballroom, the Millennium, Sagittarius, and Eternity's Children, flopped at the time of their release, but won raves from pal BRIAN WILSON and were later lavishly repackaged by ALAN McGEE's Poptones label, among others. Boettcher died, reportedly of HIV-related illness, in 1987.

Bonzo Dog Doo-Dah Band, the. English comedy collective of the sixties, enamored of Edwardian kitsch and beloved by the Beatles; they scored a U.K. Top 10 hit with the Paul McCartney–written song "I'm the Urban Spaceman." Bonzo alumnus Neil Innes went on to bigger fame as Eric Idle's collaborator on the famous Beatles parody *All You Need Is Cash*, later known simply as *The Rutles* (Innes played Ron Nasty, the Lennon character). But the most celebrated ex-Bonzo was its gonzo orange-haired frontman, Viv Stanshall, who, to the delight of romanticist Snobs, spent his post-Bonzo career behaving recklessly in grand rock-casualty style—gallivanting about London with pal Keith Moon while dressed in Nazi uniforms, ravaging himself with alcohol, and unsuccessfully attempting a Steve Winwood–assisted comeback, before literally self-immolating, dying in a suspicious house fire in 1995.

Branca, Glenn. Brash avant-rock renegade, known for composing "symphonies" for massed ranks of unconventionally tuned electric guitars, and for collaborating with like-minded unsmiling artpersons in other media, such as the choreographer Twyla Tharp and *Cremaster*-mind Matthew Barney. Despite, or perhaps because of, his irritable-janitor demeanor, Branca has been a beloved mentor to such alternative-guitar heroes as Thurston Moore and Lee Ranaldo (of the ageless upscale noiseniks SONIC YOUTH) and Helmet leader Page Hamilton.

Brill Building. Art Deco edifice in Midtown Manhattan whose spare, warren-like offices, usually outfitted with little more than a piano and two chairs, played host to two generations of important songwriters—at first, the showtunes *alter cockers* of the Broadway musical's heyday, and then, the young Jewish songwriting teams (such as Leiber and Stoller, Barry and Greenwich, Pomus and Shuman, and BACHARACH and David) whose work dominated the pop charts in the late fifties and early sixties, before the self-written songs of the Beatles and Bob Dylan deluded all youngsters into thinking they could write their own material. Snobs exult in pointing out that some of the most prominent Brill Building teams—Goffin and King, Sedaka and Greenfield, and Mann and Weil—in fact worked up the street in Don Kirshner's offices at 1650 Broadway.

Brill Building

Bubblegum. Reactionary lite-pop movement of the late sixties and early seventies instigated by record producers and songwriters who correctly deduced that there was a youthful pop audience not being served by the prevailing trends of psychedelia, POWER-TRIO blues revivalism, and nascent PROG. Bubblegum's prime movers (and namers) were the New York–based producers Jerry Kasenetz and Jeff Katz, whose Super K Records served as a vehicle for their insinuatingly catchy compositions of *Teletubbies*-level repetitiveness and simplicity, among them the Ohio Express's "Yummy Yummy Yummy" and the 1910 Fruitgum Co.'s "Simon Says." Kasenetz and Katz were eclipsed at the turn of the decade by such multimedia threats as the Partridge Family and the Osmonds, but are upheld by Snobs, paradoxically, as the "purest" of bubblegum auteurs, not least because the Ramones, ardent bubble-ologists themselves, covered the 1910 Fruitgum Co.'s "Indian Giver."

Buckingham, Lindsey. Driving musical force of the post–PETER GREEN Fleetwood Mac, once reviled by Snobs as the beardy, longhaired embodiment of complacent seventies California soft-pop, but since doubly rehabilitated—first, when he acquired an *Eraserhead* haircut and acknowledged punk and new-wave influences on both his solo albums and the Mac's admirably weird *Tusk* album; and, later, when Snobs came around to recognizing the BRIAN WILSON–like production acuity, virtuoso guitar-playing, and SUN-DRENCHED HARMONIES of his seventies Mac work. Now enjoys the friendship of such credibly hip admirers as R.E.M. and Rick Rubin.

Buckley, Tim and Jeff. Symmetrically ill-fated father-and-son artists whose early deaths, swooping voices, and Pre-Raphaelite beauty are irresistible to the romantic wing of Rock Snobbism. Jeff Buckley was eight years old when his father, a honey-voiced folkie turned jazz dabbler, died of a drug overdose, aged twenty-eight, in 1975; Buckley fils went on to become a singer-songwriter of equal repute, winning raves for his 1994 debut album, *Grace*, but drowned in Memphis, aged thirty, before he could complete a studio follow-up.

Budokan. Imposing Tokyo arena that, though built for the 1964 Olympics judo competition (its name roughly translates as "martial arts hall"), has become better known as Japan's premier rock shed. Recording a "Live at Budokan" album is a rite of passage for any artist eager to prove his popularity has gone mega, as Bob Dylan, Ozzy Osbourne, Sheryl Crow, and, especially, CHEAP TRICK would attest.

Burke, Solomon. Belatedly lionized Philadelphia soul singer. A stalwart of the fifties and sixties chitlin circuit, Burke never quite achieved the crossover success of an Otis Redding or a Ben E. King, thereby enhancing his appeal to in-the-know white hipsters. In 2002, with his moment of rediscovery at hand, the lovably eccentric Burke (who has twenty-one children and owns a chain of funeral homes) released a Snob-ratified new album whose songs were written to order by a good-taste armada that includes Elvis Costello, Bob Dylan, BRIAN WILSON, DAN PENN, Tom Waits, and Van Morrison.

Solomon Burke

Burnside, R. L. Long-serving North Mississippi bluesman who, like SOLOMON BURKE, finds himself the recipient of unforeseen September-of-his-years recognition. Chaperoned into the mainstream by the blues-revivalist FAT POSSUM label, the elderly Burnside—who literally shot and killed a man some years ago—has enjoyed newfound international exposure through his CD releases and songs licensed to *The Sopranos* and Nissan. However, illness and indifference to Greater Caucasia's adulation have limited his touring schedule.

Buster, Prince. Jamaican ska and ROCKSTEADY pioneer, born Cecil Bustamente Campbell, who wrote, produced, and performed dozens of hits in the sixties for the Blue Beat label, so much so that in England, where sharp-suited mods worshipped Buster's every move, ska was better known in some quarters as Blue Beat. Though the advent of reggae rendered Buster passé, his star rose again with the rise of JERRY DAMMERS's Two Tone label in the late seventies, most conspicuously with an onslaught of tributes from Madness, Two Tone's poppiest band, who took their name from a Prince Buster song and called their first single, in tribute, "The Prince." Buster, whose pugilistic nickname allegedly arose from his penchant for street-fighting, is now semiretired and living in Miami.

Carlos, Walter/Wendy. Modern electronic composer revered by Snobs for his/her original music for Stanley Kubrick's *A Clockwork Orange* (1971) and *The Shining* (1980), but better known to civilians as one of the world's most famous transsexuals (having undergone reassignment surgery in 1972) and as the artist behind *Switched-On Bach*, a 1968 easy-listening landmark that introduced the world to the MOOG synthesizer and ranked with the lava lamp and hanging terrarium as a seduction accessory of its time. Never a particularly mirthful figure, Carlos sued the Scottish cult performer Momus in 1999 for his tribute song, "Walter Carlos" (which imagined a romantic liaison between Walter and Wendy), but, oddly, accepted Weird Al Yankovic's invitation to collaborate on a spoof of *Peter and the Wolf.*

Wendy Carlos

Carter Family, the. Country-music dynasty whose founding members, A. P. Carter (vocals), his wife, Sara (vocals, AUTOHARP), and A.P.'s brother's wife, Maybelle (vocals, guitar), are now embraced not only by musicologists steeped in hillbilly history but, in the wake of *O Brother, Where Art Thou?* and the AMERICANA vogue, by loft dwellers who value the Virginia trio as mystical totems of that cool Dust Bowl period it's so fun to simulate by wearing overalls and calico sundresses in the farmhouse upstate.

Staples of Depression-era radio, the Carters popularized the country idiom nationwide and ushered such songs as "Keep on the Sunny Side" and "Will the Circle Be Unbroken" into the American canon. Maybelle—whom Snobs like to refer to as "Mother Maybelle" just for the sheer frisson of it—had three daughters, Helen, June, and Anita, who upheld the family tradition in the fifties and sixties as the Carter Sisters. June Carter, by marrying Johnny Cash in 1968 and uniting her progeny (among them Carlene Carter) with his (among them Rosanne Cash), perpetuated the dynasty still further. *Listening to the plain, uninflected voices of the* Carter Family *while regarding their severe, unsmiling gazes in old photographs, I get the shivers . . . like I'm receiving a transmission from a vanished world.*

Cheap Trick. Cheeseball pariahs rehabilitated by Snobs into rock's most durable POWER-POP act. Relegated to rock's second tier in the seventies, Cheap Trick finally broke big in America upon the 1979 release of their live album recorded at BUDOKAN, where Japanese youngsters still screamed like it was 1964. Nevertheless, Cheap Trick fell out of favor again as their teenybop fans grew up and tired of the band's two-freaks, two-geeks novelty image. But furtive Snob worshippers uncloseted themselves in the nineties, with STEVE ALBINI coming forward to produce the band and Smashing Pumpkins handpicking them as a support act. With even the GARAGE PUNK of the White Stripes and the Hives bearing Cheap Trick's imprimatur, the band fills ballrooms with its big-beat anthemizing to this day.

Chic. Unimpeachably upscale disco combo anchored by producer-songwriters Nile Rodgers (guitar) and Bernard

Edwards (bass). Though Chic's greatest achievements as a group came in its early years, during the 1977–79 run that produced the Studio 54 favorites "Dance, Dance, Dance (Yowsah Yowsah Yowsah)," "Le Freak," and "Good Times," Rodgers and Edwards, together and apart, enjoyed edifying postcommercial careers as producers and guest musicians, particularly in collaboration with white Englishmen besotted with Rodgers's scratchy guitar-playing and Edwards's extra-low-end bass. Among their client-fans were David Bowie, Mick Jagger, and, especially, Duran Duran, whose offshoot group the Power Station was practically a Chic tribute band (with Edwards producing and Chic drummer Tony Thompson playing). Rodgers and Edwards's work on Diana Ross's last album of any worth, *Diana* (1980), has become a Snob cause célèbre, because the willful Ross felt the Chic team overstepped its bounds and had Motown remix the album to her taste, resulting in a great "lost" mix akin to GLYN JOHNS's *Get Back* for the Beatles. Nevertheless, her hit "I'm Coming Out" bore the unmistakable Chic imprimatur, and the Rodgers-Edwards mix of *Diana* finally came out on CD in 2003 as part of Motown's Deluxe Edition of the album.

Clark, Gene. Brooding, handsome founding member of the Byrds who quit the band in 1966 after having written songs that included "Feel a Whole Lot Better" and "Eight Miles High." (Ironically, Clark's fear of flying contributed to his exit.) Subsequent albums such as *Echoes* (1967) and *No Other* (1974) achieved cult status for their audacious blend of pop, country, and gospel, and a 1968 collaboration with banjoist Doug Dillard, *The Fantastic*

Gene Clark

Expedition of Dillard & Clark, is also considered a Rock Snob classic. Entire musical careers have been constructed on emulation of Clark, in particular where the more countryish bands in the eighties PAISLEY UNDERGROUND scene were concerned. But none of Clark's albums sold beans during his lifetime, their poor commercial performance hastening his alcohol-related decline and premature death in 1991.

CMJ Music Marathon. Alternative-music trade show, held annually in New York City, that began as an outgrowth of *College Media Journal*, a college-radio trade publication founded in 1978 by young entrepreneur Robert Haber. Though more conventionally trade-showish and dorky than the SOUTH BY SOUTHWEST conference, with panels on topics like "Selecting a Manager" and "Performance Royalties," CMJ nevertheless boasts an impressive history of future-star showcases, its alumni including R.E.M. and Jane's Addiction, and affords credentialed Snobs an opportunity to quiz their favorite journalists and keynote alterna-stars up close. *My* CMJ *schedule was so busy, I had to skip the Joe Levy–Bob Christgau panel to catch the Mars Volta show.*

Cocksucker Blues. Warts-and-all documentary of the Rolling Stones' 1972 tour, directed by photographer Robert Frank and celebrated by Snobs for being very difficult to see; the Stones, having second thoughts about being captured in all their *Exile on Main Street*–era debauchery, obtained a court injunction against the film's distribution, ultimately striking an odd deal with Frank in which *Cocksucker Blues* can only be screened once a year, with the director present. Reputed to be rife with illicit orgy scenes and appalling drug abuse, the grainy, low-production-values movie is actually rather tame by today's standards, but still entertaining as an archival curio, especially in its unintentionally funny scenes depicting Bianca Jagger's existential ennui.

Cohn, Nik. Trailblazing English rock critic and self-styled street-punk author of two key Snob-lit texts, *Awopbopaloobop Alopbamboom* (1969), in which he positioned himself as one of the first critics to eulogize rock as a spent force, and *Rock Dreams* (1973), in which he wrote febrile, borderline-nonsensical captions for the artist Guy Peellaert's garish paintings of rock icons in imagined situations. Cohn's fanatical love of pinball influenced rock history when his friend Pete Townshend, incensed at Cohn's less-than-gushing assessment of an early version of *Tommy*, responded by writing "Pinball Wizard" to impress him. A few years later, Cohn once again grabbed the zeitgeist by the lapels, writing an article for *New York* magazine, "Tribal Rites of the New Saturday Night," that became the basis for the film *Saturday Night Fever*.

Cooder, Ry. Crack blues guitarist who rises above the station of mere "respected sessioneer" because of his soundtrack work (most notably for the films of Wim Wenders and Walter Hill) and his truly Snob-boggling résumé. As a teenage guitar prodigy in Los Angeles in the sixties, Cooder played on sessions for Jackie DeShannon before hooking up with the black blues-folkie Taj Mahal in the short-lived, SEMINAL blues-rock band the Rising Sons. Thereafter, Cooder, a slide virtuoso, was sought out by CAPTAIN BEEFHEART and the Rolling Stones to play on their albums. At ease, despite his scrubbed prepster appearance, in any number of ethnic idioms, Cooder is a cornerstone of the "world music" movement, having collaborated with Hawaiian, African, Japanese, and Indian musicians, and having been the prime mover behind the *Buena Vista Social Club* phenomenon, in which he gave Cuba's pre-Castro music greats (Compay Segundo, Ibrahim Ferrer, et al.) a new lease on life.

Cope, Julian. Drug-damaged but ever-chipper former leader of eighties British neo-psychedelic band the Teardrop Explodes. Whereas acid-fried Pink Floyd founder SYD BARRETT, to whom Cope is sometimes compared, has spent the years since the sixties living in grim seclusion, Cope continues to gambol merrily along, having posed naked under a giant tortoise shell on the cover of his second solo album, *Fried*, and knowingly titled a subsequent album *Droolian*. Surprisingly enterprising for a self-declared acid casualty, Cope maintains a slick Web site for fans and has written several books, including guides to KRAUTROCK and British Neolithic sites and a couple of inarguably entertaining rock memoirs.

-core. All-purpose suffix used to convey a punkish undercurrent or an extremity of vision; derived from *hardcore*, the term used to describe the California thrash-punk scene of the late seventies. *Lounge-core* describes the over-egged easy-listening vogue; *jazz-core* describes the kind of breakneck, intricate instrumental music that Frank Zappa played on his excursions into jazz territory; *emo-core* enjoyed a brief vogue as a term for sensitive-but-punk-steeped music for depressive teens, before being superseded by the more succinct term EMO.

Coruscating. Critic-beloved adjective, literally meaning "giving forth flashes of light; sparkling," that is invariably used to describe guitar solos or riffs. *John Frusciante turns in some* coruscating *guitar work on the new Chili Peppers album.*

Cosmic. Musically meaningless adjective deployed by rock writers to ascribe a mysterious otherness to the actually quite straightforward country music played by GRAM PARSONS and other lysergically inclined, NUDIE-suited, anti-Nashville mavericks in the late sixties and early seventies; derived from Parsons's resistance of the term "country rock" and insistence that what he played was, in fact, "cosmic American music." The term was repurposed in the eighties to describe the anthemic "big music" of such British groups as the Waterboys, the Alarm, Simple Minds, and early U2. *The* Grievous Angel *album represents the apotheosis of Parsons's* cosmic *vision.*

Countrypolitan. Slick, orchestrally layered country music, denuded of country's hillbilly, honky-tonk heritage, that held sway in the late sixties and seventies under the aegis of the producer Billy Sherrill, a sort of Nashville analogue to Phil Spector. Though Sherrill's productions for George Jones, Tanya Tucker, Charlie Rich, and Tammy Wynette (for whom he wrote "Stand By Your Man") are antithetical to the ROOTS-based approach generally favored by Snobs, the countrypolitan era is nevertheless held in high Snob esteem for its emotionally fraught balladry and JACK NITZSCHE–worthy arrangements. In 1981, as he neared retirement, a bemused Sherrill obliged Elvis Costello's request that he man the boards for the former new-waver's country album, *Almost Blue.*

THE GODFATHER GUIDE

Godfathers of Funk

James Brown
George Clinton
Bootsy Collins
Lee Dorsey

Godfathers of Grunge

The Pixies
The Replacements
Neil Young and Crazy Horse
Hüsker Dü
Killing Joke

Godfathers of Hip-Hop

DJ Kool Herc
Afrika Bambaataa
Grandmaster Flash
Grand Wizard Theodore
Gil Scott-Heron
The Last Poets
Amiri Baraka (aka LeRoi Jones)

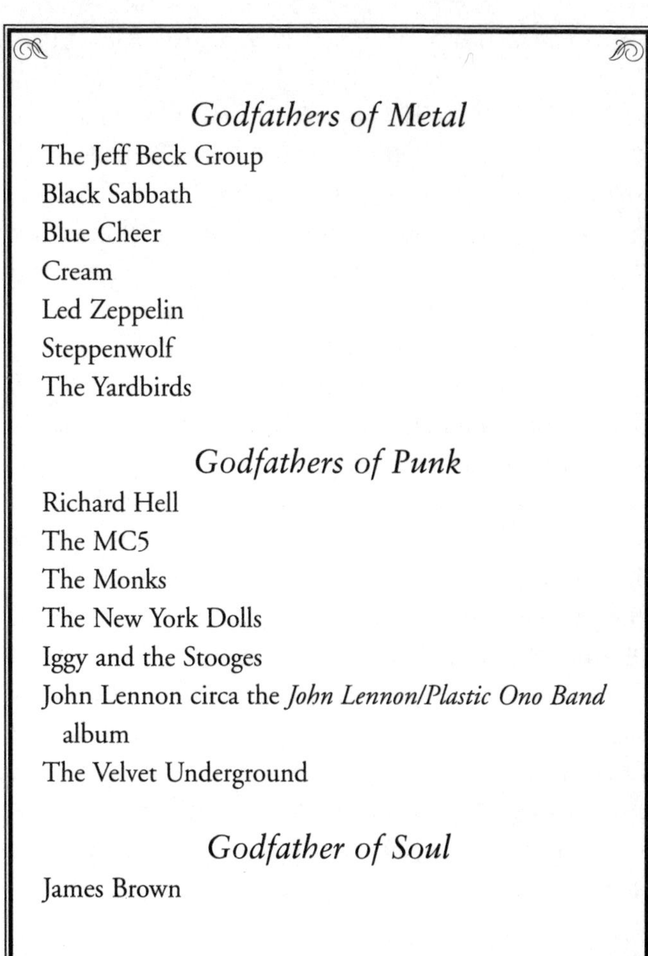

Godfathers of Metal

The Jeff Beck Group
Black Sabbath
Blue Cheer
Cream
Led Zeppelin
Steppenwolf
The Yardbirds

Godfathers of Punk

Richard Hell
The MC5
The Monks
The New York Dolls
Iggy and the Stooges
John Lennon circa the *John Lennon/Plastic Ono Band* album
The Velvet Underground

Godfather of Soul

James Brown

Crawdaddy! The first mainstream rock magazine, founded in New York in 1966, a year before *Rolling Stone*, by Paul Williams. Though it ceased publication in 1979, Williams revived it as a newsletter in 1993. Just about every major rock biography seems to rely heavily on ancient *Crawdaddy!* interviews.

Crazy Horse. Neil Young's fiery backing band, on and off, since 1969. Frequently held up, along with relative youngsters THE REPLACEMENTS and THE PIXIES, as progenitors of grunge, Crazy Horse (drummer Ralph Molina, bassist Billy Talbot, and guitarist Frank "Poncho" Sampedro, who replaced heroin casualty Danny Whitten) are revered by graying Snobs for their emotional playing and frayed-denim-and-flannelly-paunch integrity.

Crowley, Aleister. Suave gentleman Satanist (1875–1947) who stands second only to Charles Manson as the mascot of choice for danger-craving bad-boy rockers. From the early twentieth century until his death, Crowley quilled messianic tracts about "magick," a crepuscular practice that, though it held little entertainment value, proved seductive to impressionable rockers like the Beatles, who included Crowley's face on the cover of *Sgt. Pepper*, and Led Zeppelin's Jimmy Page, who purchased Crowley's old estate in Scotland and is the world's premier collector of Crowley memorabilia. Crowley's rock acolytes haven't been deterred, and may indeed be encouraged, by scholarly suggestions that his dabblings in the black arts were really a clever front for a libertine kink 'n' coke lifestyle.

Dammers, Jerry. Career-stunted pop visionary and musical mastermind behind the Specials, the multiracial ska revivalists who, from 1979 to 1981, scored a string of sardonic hits in Britain, and whose debut album was Snob-ratified by producer Elvis Costello. As the proprietor of independent Two Tone label (Madness, the [English] Beat), Dammers, known for his geniality and missing incisors, was widely expected to become a

Jerry Dammers

major musical force in Britain, yet, after the original Specials split, he fell prey to BRIAN WILSON–like perfectionism and produced little apart from the human-rights anthem "Free Nelson Mandela." Romanticized as the Snob Prince who abdicated, Dammers today subsists on DJing jobs and what-might-have-been mystique.

Dean, Roger. Airbrush-wielding maestro behind such PROG-tastic album covers as Yes's *Close to the Edge* and *Tales from Topographic Oceans* and Asia's eponymous debut. Nearly as revered by cover-art nerds as the HIPGNOSIS team, and second to no one in having his artwork copied onto the sides of vans.

Debussy, Claude. French composer of the late nineteenth and early twentieth century who felt a greater kinship with the Impressionist poets and painters of his day than with traditional classical composers. His deeply felt, impressionistic music, full of unusual harmonies and sensitive dynamics, has colored (or, better perhaps, "coloured") the work of experimentalist popsters from the Beatles, whose "Strawberry Fields Forever" was described by its producer, George Martin, as "a complete tone poem—like a modern Debussy" to the electro-pop pranksters the Art of Noise, who released a tribute album entitled *The Seduction of Claude Debussy* in 1999.

Delaney and Bonnie. Frye-booted, syphilitic-looking married couple of early-seventies vintage (last name: Bramlett) who pioneered the "heavy friends" approach to a rock career, recording several albums of amiable but undistinguished blues chooglin' in the company of such esteemed helpers as Eric Clapton, Duane Allman, George

Harrison, and Dave Mason. (Their best-known album is called *Delaney & Bonnie & Friends on Tour with Eric Clapton.*) Though their time in the spotlight was short-lived, Bonnie Bramlett resurfaced in the late seventies when she clocked Elvis Costello in a bar fight.

Detroit techno. Underground movement that fused black funk and soul music to the robotic-futurist stylings of KRAFTWERK, resulting in an elaborate, storied subculture that bypassed most Americans but became hugely influential in Europe and in Snob circles, where it is de rigueur to know the names of Detroit techno pioneers Derrick May and Juan Atkins. Influenced by Charles Johnson, a Motor City DJ of the late seventies and early eighties who called himself the Electrifyin' Mojo and played an eclectic mix of Eurodisco, U.S. funk, KRAUTROCK, and British new wave on his show, May, Atkins, and their compatriots forged a new genre—abetted by the new affordability of such drum machines as the ROLAND 808—that sounded, in May's words, "like George Clinton and Kraftwerk stuck in an elevator." Subsequent waves of Detroiters have taken up the May-Atkins mantle and received lucrative commissions from Belgian clubs and British advertising agencies. *The 1992 release of Carl Craig's "Bug in a Bassbin" was a clarion call for the second wave of* Detroit techno.

Dexys Midnight Runners. English pop group known to civilians as the one-hit wonders behind the 1982 song "Come On Eileen" but to Snobs as the vehicle of the audacious musical maverick and street tough Kevin Rowland, who led the band through three distinct incarnations. The first, as featured on the 1979 album

Searching for the Young Soul Rebels, was a horn-driven NORTHERN SOUL refutation of Rowland's punk-rock origins; the second, as featured on 1982's *Too-Rye-Ay*, was the scruffy, fiddle-y, banjo-pickin', overalls-wearin', shirt-shunnin' approach familiar to early-MTV viewers; the third, as featured on 1984's *Don't Stand Me Down*, was a critic-baiting hodgepodge of evangelical keening and Beckettesque spoken interludes, its weirdness compounded by Rowland's perverse Brooks Brothers makeover of the band (madras shorts, plaid blazers, rep ties, Golden Fleece polos, etc.). Though Rowland today is considered a damaged nut job—he appeared on the cover of his 1999 album, *My Beauty*, in a dress and garters, apparently sincere in his desire to look sexy—*Don't Stand Me Down* was reappraised upon its CD reissue as a work of genius by Britain's last great pop auteur.

Dickinson, Jim. Mainstay musician-producer of the Memphis scene since the sixties, notable for his Zelig-like penchant for turning up at particularly Snob-worthy moments in rock history—he played piano on the Rolling Stones' "Wild Horses," produced BIG STAR's records, sessioned on Aretha Franklin and Sam & Dave songs for Atlantic Records, and did soundtrack work with RY COODER in the eighties, all the while enjoying an edifying side career as a solo practitioner of SOUTHERN-FRIED BOOGIE. Wins further Snob points for having fathered Luther and Cody Dickinson, leaders of the Snob-approved band the North Mississippi Allstars, and for frequently being confused with Byrds svengali producer Jim Dickson.

Jim Dickinson

Dion. Bronx-born tenor-survivor—full name Dion DiMucci—fetishized by Snobs not so much for his late-fifties tenure in the Belmonts ("A Teenager in Love") or his early-sixties solo stardom ("The Wanderer") as for his patchy later career. Thanks to a serious heroin habit, Dion took a five-year furlough from the business before reemerging in 1968, Bobby Darin–style, as a sincere folkie. A subsequent incarnation as a street poet (tweed pimp hats à la Springsteen) was less fruitful. The CD reissue of Dion's uneven, long-out-of-print 1975 album *Born to Be with You*—produced by Phil Spector when both men couldn't get arrested commercially—has prompted flailing spasms of rock-crit overpraise.

DJ Kool Herc. Hulking, dreadlocked Jamaican expat known to all Snobs as the true originator of hip-hop, predating even the Kangol-capped DJs and MCs of the genre's OLD SCHOOL. In the early seventies, Herc, who was born Clive Campbell in Kingston and nicknamed Hercules in his Bronx high school for his athletic prowess, started DJing at block parties. Attempting to re-create the DUB-style rhythmic sparseness he remembered from parties in his homeland, Herc set up two turntables side by side, enabling him to run together rhythmic breaks, or break beats, from two copies of the same arcane SIDE—establishing the foundation, figuratively and sonically, of hip-hop. (Herc enlisted an MC named Coke La Rock to rap lines like "Ya rock and ya don't stop," and later traveled from party to party with a whole posse of "Herculoids.") A recalcitrant individual who has seldom recorded, Herc has enhanced his Snob cred by keeping a low profile.

Dobro. Brand name for a family of hollow-bodied, heavily ornamented resonator guitars developed in California in the twenties. Long beloved by country, blues, and bluegrass players for their metallic, extra-twangy sound and gorgeous circular cover plates, Dobros are increasingly valued by rock-country hybridists like WILCO, Ryan Adams, and Lucinda Williams, especially the square-necked models, which afford a musician the priceless ROOTS-sensitive visual opportunity to play a guitar horizontally in one's lap.

Dobro

Dolby 5.1. Sophisticated digital audio format that has leapt from movie theaters to home theaters with the advent of digital cable television and the DVD, offering five main channels (left, center, right, left surround, and right surround) plus an extra dedicated channel (the ".1") for low-range bass effects. Archivist Snobs are now scrambling to repurchase all their favorite concert films, rockumentaries, and propulsively soundtracked Scorsese flicks in 5.1 to get the full, visceral experience the artists intended. *When the hell are they going to put out Nic Roeg's* Performance *in* Dolby 5.1*?*

Don Kirshner's Rock Concert. Syndicated television program that was a staple of Saturday-night (actually Sunday-at-1 a.m.) teen viewing in the seventies, before MTV existed. Though the middle-aged, comb-over'd Kirshner, a BRILL BUILDING–era music publisher and the show's executive producer, was a stiflingly acharismatic and untelegenic host (famously parodied by Paul Shaffer on

Saturday Night Live), *Rock Concert* offered underage rock fans then-rare opportunities to witness pre-taped yet un-lip-sync'd performances by such musicians as Neil Young, Kiss, the late-period, hairy Byrds, and even the Sex Pistols, THE NEW YORK DOLLS, Patti Smith, and SPARKS.

Dorsey, Lee. Natty, smooth-voiced New Orleans R&B singer of short-lived chart success (1961–66) but long-term Snob exaltedness, exhumed from obscurity to open for the Clash in 1980 (he'd been working as an auto mechanic) and given the full SUNDAZED reissue treatment in recent times. Though best known for his peppy 1961 novelty hit "Ya Ya," Dorsey later moved into proto-funk, thus earning him a namecheck in the Beastie Boys' "Sure Shot," in which Michael Diamond boasts, "Everything I do is funky like Lee Dorsey."

Drake, Nick. Sad-sack, compulsively muted English singer-songwriter from posh background, posthumously canonized by Rock Snobs for the three plaintive, delicately wrought albums he recorded before dying, an apparent suicide, in 1974 at the age of twenty-six. Was frequently photographed standing dolefully among trees. Achieved a measure of posthumous fame when his song "Pink Moon" was used in a Volkswagen TV commercial.

Dr. John. Stage name for New Orleans singer-pianist Mac Rebennack, be-plumed overlord of "voodoo rock." Struggling as an R&B musician in his hometown, Rebennack headed out west in the mid-sixties and found work as a member of Sonny & Cher's touring band before coming up with a loony alter ego that, wittingly or not, dovetailed perfectly with the psychedelic craze: Dr. John the Night Tripper, a character named after a real nineteenth-century Haitian voodoo doctor and decked out in a feathered headdress, cape, and face paint. Rebennack's 1968 debut as Dr. John, *Gris-Gris*, was a shiveringly spooky amalgam of blues, soul, R&B, and drug-alteredness that evinced an authentic swamp vibe, even though it was actually recorded in the Los Angeles studio where Phil Spector produced his girl-group hits. Rebennack has since gone through many phases, including a funkified one with THE METERS as his backing band and a more recent one as an interpreter of standards, but nevertheless triggers in Snobs involuntary usage of the *Gris-Gris*–redolent terms "gumbo," "N'awlins," and "the good doctor's remedy."

Dub. Term originally used to denote the music on B sides of early reggae singles, which featured a bass-heavy remix of the A side with the vocal track eliminated. Later expanded to encompass any sparse, rhythm-centric reggae production that leaves plenty of room on top for toasting, rapping, poetry recital, and other forms of show-offy noodlage. A nonchalantly displayed grasp of the difference between dub and other reggae-related formats (dancehall, ROOTS, skinhead, ROCKSTEADY) is compulsory for Caucasian Rasta Snobs.

Dub plate. Custom-made one-off vinyl discs whose origins date back to Jamaica's fiercely competitive reggae scene of the sixties. An even hotter commodity than a WHITE LABEL, a dub plate is a special mix that goes straight from the studio to the DJ, who boasts loudly of his exclusive. The Rock Snob, unless he is Island Records founder Chris Blackwell or an actual Jamaican, has never handled and never will handle a "dub plate special," but it is incumbent upon him to nod knowingly at the mention of the term.

Durutti Column, the. Mysterious nom-de-band for alarmingly gaunt English guitarist Vini Reilly, whose 1980 debut, *The Return of the Durutti Column*, issued by Manchester's storied Factory Records (Joy Division, Happy Mondays), showcased a suite of lush, effects-heavy instrumentals that were incongruously chilled-out for the POST-PUNK times. Though he flirted with commerciality in 1988 when he contributed to Morrissey's album *Viva Hate*, Reilly is generally content to release harmless, uninteresting albums to a bijou following.

Dury, Ian. Endearing Cockney unusualist who emerged from the PUB ROCK mire at age thirty-five to become an unlikely star in the punk era. His growth stunted by a childhood bout of polio that also left one leg withered, Dury broke through with his 1977 album *New Boots and Panties!!*, a collection of funky low-life vignettes delivered in an offhand *sprech-stimme* style and underpinned, almost daringly for punk times, by the adept musicianship of his seasoned backing band, the Blockheads. An adroit lyricist, Dury gave the world the phrases (as well as the songs) "Sex & Drugs & Rock & Roll," "Reasons to Be Cheerful," and "Hit Me with Your Rhythm Stick." *The world's a darker place now that Lord Upminster himself,* Ian Dury, *has shuffled this mortal coil.*

Earle, Steve. World-weary singer-songwriter, hailed in Rock Snob circles as the only contemporary country artist (as opposed to ALT.COUNTRY artist) fit to polish Hank Williams's cowboy boots. Earle made a triumphant debut with his 1986 album, *Guitar Town*, only to fritter away his early promise on a five-year drugs-and-drink bender. Now clean, burly, and middle-aged, he inspires a Springsteen-like reverence among fans and critics, both for his storytellin' songs and his impassioned political positions, such as his anti–death penalty stance.

Steve Earle

Easy listening. The most apropos of the unofficial umbrella terms for the multiple permutations of mid-century or mid-century-imitative soft pop in Snob vogue since the nineties: lounge-core, space-age-bachelor-pad music, JIMMY WEBB's songs for the Fifth Dimension, just about anything by BURT BACHARACH, etc. A problematic term in that it's employed contemptuously in some quarters and with rectorial earnestness in others.

Eat the Document. Unreleased documentary of Bob Dylan's tumultuous 1966 world tour with the Hawks (later to be known as the Band), filmed, like the previous year's Dylan doc, *Don't Look Back*, by D. A. Pennebaker, but this time in color and edited in nonlinear, "impressionistic" fashion by Dylan himself. Commissioned as a TV special for ABC but shelved for being too weird, *Eat the Document*, like *COCKSUCKER BLUES*, remains extraordinarily difficult to see—literally so in the poor-quality bootlegs in wide circulation. Even the "official" version occasionally screened in museums and art-house theaters omits all but seconds of the film's most famous footage, of competitor-compatriots Dylan and John Lennon tensely trading shtick in the back of a limo in London before Dylan, haggard and ill, retches into the camera.

E-bow. Guitarist's gadget that allows the player to create eerie drones and cello-like sustains. Introduced in the mid-seventies, the e-bow is a small handheld box that, when placed near a guitar's strings, creates a magnetic field that results in a feedback-like wail that's more controllable than actual feedback. The eighties Scottish group Big Country used the e-bow to create its trademark "bagpipey guitar" sound, while Peter Buck used the device on R.E.M.'s least-enjoyable single, named, in tribute, "E-Bow the Letter."

Einstürzende Neubauten. POST-PUNK German avant-gardists more beloved by Snobs for their comically cumbersome name (which translates roughly to "imploding new buildings"), and their incorporation of such industrial implements as jackhammers, power drills, and circular saws into their music, than for their percussive but ultimately tedious clatter. The concept of Einstürzende Neubaten was ultimately more entertainingly realized by such family-friendly off-Broadway attractions as *Stomp!* and the Blue Man Group.

Electroclash. Assaultive, hokey club-music trendlet with wishfully grandiose name. Posited as the music of the twenty-second century by warehouse-club folk and newspaper style sections, Electroclash, as practiced by New York City standard-bearers Fischerspooner and A.R.E. Weapons, amounts to little more than eighties-style synth-and-beat-box music played in art galleries while its practitioners stage street-theater "happenings" that owe more to mime and *Xena, Warrior Princess* than Velvets subversiveness or Warholian spark.

Emo. Controversial term for a strain of punk-steeped yet thoughtful rock popular among depressive teens and twenty-somethings. Arising out of a Washington, D.C., scene of the mid-eighties in which hardcore bands got tired of playing noise and went slightly sensitive and midtempo, emo matured into a codified national movement in the late nineties with such bands as Jimmy Eat World and Promise Ring, which played pained hard rock overlaid with boyish vocals characterized by odd, flatulent vowel pronunciations. By the turn of the century, emo had broadened in scope to accommodate the maudlin Dashboard Confessional, the somewhat more jaundiced Cursive and Yellowcard, and the countryish Bright Eyes. Aptly, given the hypersensitivity of the genre's practitioners, most emo artists recoil at being called "emo," claim that their music is unique and uncategorizable, and insist that you don't even know what the term means anyway.

Eno, Brian. Egghead producer and electronics whiz with appropriately futuristic name and aerodynamic pate. Eno started out as the keyboard player for ROXY MUSIC and went on to make his name as a producer (Talking Heads, Devo, U2) and pioneer of ambient music, the soundtrack for everything from aromatherapy to recreational drug use to booting up Windows 95. Eno enjoys his greatest Rock Snob status, however, for his seventies solo albums, *Another Green World, Here Come the Warm Jets, Taking Tiger Mountain (By Strategy)*, and *Before and After Science.*

Brian Eno

Erickson, Roky. Texas psychedelia kingpin often championed, like SKIP SPENCE, as North America's answer to SYD BARRETT. The oddball lead singer of the 13th Floor Elevators, Erickson was arrested for possession of drugs in 1968. Attempting to avoid jail time, he pleaded insanity and was committed to Texas's Rusk State Hospital for the Criminally Insane, where electroshock therapy exacerbated his eccentric tendencies more than drugs ever did. Erickson now lives under his family's supervision in Austin, occasionally recording gonzo albums that actually get decent reviews.

ESG. Anomalous black female NO WAVE outfit from the South Bronx that, at the dawn of the eighties, captivated obtuse artpersons both in Downtown Manhattan and in Manchester, England's burgeoning POST-PUNK scene. Signed to Manchester's SEMINAL Factory Records label, sisters Renee, Marie, Valerie, and Deborah Scroggins produced a strange amalgam of funky bass, punkish vocalizing, and skeletal, ambient arrangements. The sparseness of ESG's records made them ideal for sampling and rapping over, a circumstance that OLD-SCHOOL hip-hoppers took copious advantage of, and that the Scroggins sisters mordantly reflected upon in the title of one of their comeback albums, *Sample Credits Don't Pay Our Bills.*

Ezrin, Bob. Astute hard-rock producer who specialized in greasepaint bombast (Kiss, Alice Cooper) but detoured into arty music, most celebratedly on Lou Reed's *Berlin* and the first of Peter Gabriel's eponymous solo albums (aka the "Rainy Car" album). Ezrin's melding of kickass production and cerebral theatricality reached its apex on Pink Floyd's *The Wall*, on which he was effectively a fifth member of the fractious band (reprising his "School's Out" trick of using a kids' chorus on "Another Brick in the Wall"), and on Kiss's then-reviled but since Snob-reappraised 1981 "conceptual" album, *Music from "The Elder,"* to which Reed also contributed.

Fairlight. Australian-manufactured synthesizer that was de rigueur for any eighties artist wishing to sound futuristic. Avid Fairlight users included Peter Gabriel, Thomas Dolby, Alan Parsons, Herbie Hancock, and *Miami Vice* composer Jan Hammer. Though Fairlights came to be reviled in the purist climate of grunge and classic rock, they fetch top dollar from Vintage Equipment Snobs who value their kitschy prerecorded samples and now retro sound. *Doing that Missy Elliott remix was the perfect excuse for me to use that hilarious cor anglais sample on my old* Fairlight.

Faithfull, Marianne. Marlboro-voiced pop survivor who has shed her earlier incarnations—as the English-rose chanteuse of the baroque-pop Jagger-Richards song "As Tears Go By" and the wasted Rolling Stones concubine who inspired and cowrote "Sister Morphine"—to become the witty, Weimarish den mama of indiedom. Having first gone down this path with 1979's comeback LP, *Broken English*, Faithfull cashed in her formidable equity as a Rock Snob icon by recording her 2002 album, *Kissin' Time*, with top-ranking collaborators Beck, Billy Corgan, and Jarvis Cocker.

Marianne Faithfull

Fanny. Short-lived all-female Californian rock band from the early seventies, retroactively accorded significance in the nineties by chroniclers of the grrrl-rock "revolution." Though neither critics nor the American public particularly cared for the group's lumpen hard rock, Fanny's five albums fared slightly better in Britain, where "fanny" is slang for vagina.

Farina, Richard and Mimi. Star-crossed sixties folk legends of intriguingly slim recorded legacy. The Brooklyn-born Richard was an impossibly romantic figure who ran guns for the Irish Republican Army in the fifties, joined the Cuban revolution, befriended Thomas Pynchon in college, and so impressed Bob Dylan in his Greenwich Village folkie days that ZIMMY is said to have appropriated Richard's ice-cool persona wholesale. Richard recorded two dulcimer-infused, well-received albums with his second wife, Mimi, Joan Baez's younger sister, before dying in a 1966 motorcycle crash. A widow at twenty-one, Mimi never again regained her career momentum and died of cancer in 2001, just as interest in her early work was reviving.

Fat Possum. Oxford, Mississippi–based blues-revivalist label whose white founder, Matthew Johnson, has adeptly exhumed such aged but sentient bluesmen as R. L. BURNSIDE and T-Model Ford from obscurity, committing their songs to CD and packaging the results with a nod to the authenticity-hungry AMERICANA market; Ford, for example, is described in his album notes as having "ankles [that] wear the ragged scars of chain gang shackles." Fat Possum has also entered the GARAGE PUNK fray by signing the White Stripes–ish guitar-drums duo the Black Keys.

Fender Rhodes. Electric piano with resonant, fuzzy timbre that bestows instant sensitivity upon its user. Originally a jazz-club staple, the Rhodes became ubiquitous in the squishy mid-seventies, appearing on everything from jazz-rock fuzak albums to the Rolling Stones' "Fool to Cry," and has recently been revived by mood-music trendsetters such as Air.

Fields, Danny. Epoch-, genre-, and coast-straddling rock scenester. As an Elektra Records "house freak" in the late sixties, Fields piloted Jim Morrison through interviews in Los Angeles and traveled to Detroit to sign the proto-punks the MC5 to the label. Further demonstrating his keen eye for credible lost causes, he then went on to manage both THE STOOGES and Boston's Modern Lovers. Prudently maintaining a side gig in journalism, Fields improbably installed himself as the editor of the New York–based teenybop magazine *Sixteen* in the mid-seventies, interviewing the likes of the Bay City Rollers even as he buttressed his punk cred by taking on the Ramones as management clients. In 2000, Fields reverted to fandom with a widely reviled biography of his late friend Linda McCartney.

Flaming Lips, the. Late-blooming Oklahoma-based rock group, around long enough to have opened for the SEMINAL eighties hardcore and punk-pop bands Black Flag, Hüsker Dü, and the Butthole Surfers, but now at the vanguard of a widescreen-psychedelia movement that also includes Mercury Rev and the Polyphonic Spree. Gradually sloughing off their scuzz-rock origins, the Lips won minor recognition for their hit "She Don't Use Jelly" in 1994, before hitting the Snob mother lode with their melodious quasi-concept albums *The Soft Bulletin* (1999) and *Yoshimi Battles the Pink Robots* (2002), which have turned their front man, the adorable, prematurely gray Wayne Coyne, into the Justin Timberlake of the Volvo-owning set.

A GUIDE TO SNOB NOMENCLATURE

How to Correctly Identify Esteemed Rock Personages in Conversation with Other Snobs

"Zimmy," not "Bob" or "Dylan" (for Bob Dylan)

"Jim," not "Iggy" (for Iggy Pop, né James Osterberg)

"Mo," not "Maureen" Tucker (for the Velvet Underground's drummer)

"Moe," not "Moses" Asch (Folkways Records founder)

"Bam," not "Afrika" Bambaataa (for the hip-hop pioneer)

"Ronnie" or "Woody," not "Ron" Wood (for the Rolling Stones' junior guitarist)

"Percy," not "Robert" Plant (for Led Zeppelin's lead singer)

"Our Kid," not "Liam Gallagher" (for Oasis's lead singer)

"Nez," not "Michael Nesmith" (for the ex-Monkee and country-rock visionary)

"Lord Upminster," not "Ian Dury" (for the beloved Cockney poet-singer)

"The 'Mats," not "The Replacements" (derived from "The Placemats," band nickname used by diehard fans)

Flange. Common pedal-activated effect that produces a "whooshy" sound in any instrument through which it is processed. Snobs employ this term to show off their ability to pronounce it correctly ("flanj," not "flaing") and their versedness in FX terminology. *The Flaming Lips' "The Spiderbite Song" announces itself in a hail of heavily* flanged *drums.*

Flatlanders, the. Lubbock, Texas–based country-rock combo that split up shortly after the release of their eponymous debut album in 1972, posthumously earning plaudits as a SEMINAL influence on AMERICANA. Core members Joe Ely, Butch Hancock, and Jimmie Dale Gilmore went on to enjoy crit-coddled solo careers—Ely as a Clash-endorsed ROOTS rocker, Hancock as a cowboy poet, Gilmore as a campus-friendly hippie shaman—before recombining in the twenty-first century for a feel-good, wrinklier-but-wiser second go-round.

Folkways Records. Encyclopedic folk and world-music label founded in 1948 by Moses Asch, a recording engineer and devout socialist; now administered by the Smithsonian Institution. Beyond issuing *THE ANTHOLOGY OF AMERICAN FOLK MUSIC*, Asch, who defined folk music as "anything that is sound," released an eclectic array of titles ranging from *Lappish Joik Songs from Northern Norway* and *Six Toronto Poets* to the more expected Woody Guthrie–type fare. Snobs value vintage Folkways releases for their durability (Asch didn't scrimp on the heavy-duty vinyl) and for their inclusion of extensive booklets rather than mere sleeve notes, a practice that wasn't picked up by other labels until the CD-reissue era.

Fowley, Kim. Vampiric mainstay of the Sunset Strip scene; the Robert Evans of sleaze-pop. Born to a Hollywood family in 1942—his father, Douglas, played Doc Holliday on TV's *Wyatt Earp*—Fowley, a strikingly tall, spindly figure and gifted BS artist, hustled his way into the music business in the early sixties, actually managing to produce two Top 5 novelty singles in that era, the Hollywood Argyles' "Alley-Oop" and the Murmaids' "Popsicles and Icicles." Thereafter, he earned scenester credentials as a Frank Zappa acolyte and freak-about-town, theatrically flailing his long limbs on the dancefloors of L.A.'s newly druggy clubs. Since the sixties, Fowley has gained modest renown as an eccentric solo artist and minor-league producer, most notoriously as the man who manufactured the bad-girl group THE RUNAWAYS in the mid-seventies. But he's found his true calling in recent decades as a glib, gossipy quote machine, making creepy, flat-affect appearances in film documentaries and E! television programs about Hollywood sordidness.

Frame, Pete. Rock genealogist and founder of the English rock magazine *Zigzag*. Frame got the idea in 1971 to illustrate rock-band histories in family-tree form: explanatory text and diagrams rendered in Frame's scrawly, homely hand, depicting a progenitor band's mutation into spin-off bands, solo sojourns, and supergroups. (Blood, Sweat & Tears was the first subject.) Frame's family trees have since blossomed into a cottage industry, with books, TV shows, and, for a time, a monthly "Family Twig" feature in MOJO.

Free Design, the. Diabetic-endangering vocal group from the late sixties whose unspeakably sugary music has been aggressively revivified by loonily devoted Japanese fans, American EASY LISTENING evangelists, and such hipster acolytes as the Anglo-French soft-pop band Stereolab. A sort of proto–Starland Vocal Band but with even more Muzaky flourishes and nicey-nicey lyrics—its most famous and representative song is called "Kites Are Fun"—the Free Design, a coed collection of siblings from upstate New York, re-formed in 2000 to capitalize on the new interest, releasing an album winkingly entitled *Cosmic Peekaboo*.

Fripp, Robert. Tiny British guitar god of nutty-professor mien. Having emerged in the late sixties as the maestro of the compulsively time-signature-shifting PROG pioneers King Crimson, Fripp allied himself in the seventies with ROXY MUSIC refugee BRIAN ENO, who enlisted his friend to contribute a couple days' worth of "Frippertronics"—the swirling, densely harmonic guitar sound the pair had developed together—to David Bowie's *Heroes*. Fripp's crucial contribution to Bowie's peak achievement has earned him bulletproof status in Snob circles, despite such post-Eno taste lapses as his sundry attempts to retool King Crimson for the high-tech, post-patchouli age, and his appearance, in a *Hello!*-magazine photo spread, clinking champagne glasses in the bathtub with his wife, former eighties punk-pop oddity turned TV personality Toyah Wilcox.

Robert Fripp

Frisell, Bill. Bespectacled nice-guy guitar god of avant-jazz. As a charter member of the eighties good-taste epidemic, wherein the gaudy excesses of the seventies (PROG, jazz fusion, long hair) were traded in for adventurous musical experimentation as pursued by virtuoso, pleasant-looking young men (see also THE KNITTING FACTORY and SONIC YOUTH), Frisell has built up a loyal following of self-described "Billheads" who enthusiastically join him on his cross-genre treks into bluegrass, country, TRAD JAZZ, pop, film scoring (he wrote new soundtracks to Buster Keaton's old silents), and ambient. His fluid playing and catholic taste have earned him admission into HAL WILLNER's Rock Snob clubhouse, where he has collaborated with the likes of Elvis Costello, MARIANNE FAITHFULL, and good-taste-epidemic saxophonist John Zorn.

Fugs, the. Satirist-anarchist New York City "rock" group that arose in 1964 from the embers of the Beat movement, anchored by Ed Sanders, a poet and owner of the Peace Eye Book Store in the East Village, and Tuli Kupferberg, a poet of advanced age (he was already forty-two when the group started up) and no innate musical ability but plentiful moxie and vim. Setting their hash-steeped, filthy lyrics ("Her pelvis got the caffeine shakes/ Come on down for an ice cream soda/ I just got a Coca-Cola douche") to a willfully LO-FI sound, the Fugs, in concept and hirsute appearance, anticipated such wiseguy acts as Frank Zappa and the Mothers and CAPTAIN BEEFHEART, though without the misanthropy and aggressively show-offy musicality. Like Kiss, the Fugs continue to play farewell gigs without actually going away.

Fuzzbox. Succinctly named effects pedal of antediluvian vintage. When it first appeared in the sixties, the fuzzbox incited a new stage in rock's evolution, enabling guitarists to swathe their licks in unprecedentedly menacing distortion, a quality that appealed to the histrionic Pete Townshend, who embraced the Colorsound Tone Bender model in 1965, and the occultist Jimmy Page, who used the fuzzbox on Led Zeppelin's early albums. Though comically low-tech by modern standards, the fuzzbox is affectionately regarded by Equipment Snobs and was briefly revived in the eighties by the one-joke U.K. girl band We've Got a Fuzzbox and We're Gonna Use It.

Gainsbourg, Serge. Raffish, *joli laid* French balladeer revered by kitsch-loving Rock Snobs for his sleazy-listening pop of the sixties and seventies. Despite hangdog looks and an inability to actually sing, Gainsbourg embodied the pungent flower of French manhood in all its Gallic glory, duetting and getting busy with such hotties of the period as Brigitte Bardot and English dolly bird Jane Birkin. A less edifying collaboration was 1984's "Lemon Incest," a duet with his then-twelve-year-old daughter, Charlotte. Gainsbourg died in 1991, five years after saying "I want to *fouck* her" while sitting beside Whitney Houston on a live talk show.

Gang of Four. English band of the late seventies and early eighties that, like WIRE, caused critics to involuntarily use the words POST-PUNK and "angular." Though the band's Marxist politics (as underscored by their Sino-historical name) found few followers beyond the future members of Rage Against the Machine, Gang of Four's sparse, funkified twitch-rock sound remains heavily influential, from those who evoke it knowingly (the Red Hot Chili Peppers) to those who evoke it unknowingly (Limp Bizkit). In keeping with the times, Gang of Four's original lineup has recently reunited to belatedly reap the benefits of having been SEMINAL.

Garage punk. Halfhearted, that'll-do term for the onslaught of "the" bands (the Hives, the Strokes, the White Stripes, the

Vines, the Raveonettes, and, er, "the" Yeah Yeah Yeahs) that have risen in skinny-trousered rebellion against the *Total Request Live*–teenybop hegemony of the late twentieth century. Most garage-punk bands combine a fealty to NUGGETS-style LO-FI rambunctiousness with a preening visual presentation that borrows heavily from NO WAVE.

Glam. Glitter-dusted rock subgenre of the early seventies, built around outlandish, sexually ambiguous visuals (platform shoes, grape-snuggler tights, mime-ish face paint) as much as on its musical principles of shouty, singalong choruses and simple guitar riffs. Instigated by T. REX's Marc Bolan, glam reached its commercial and artistic apex with David Bowie's copper-mulleted Ziggy Stardust persona, and also yielded such second-rank hitmakers as Slade, the Sweet, Gary Glitter, and Mott the Hoople. In America, glam took on a darker, urban, rough-trade air as practitioned by THE NEW YORK DOLLS and Lou Reed in his homosexual phase, though mensch-glamster Alice Cooper made the genre palatable for suburbanites.

Goldman, Albert. Elfin, dyspeptic rock biographer and Snob piñata. In the 1960s, Goldman, a former classical-music academic, was the resident pop critic for *Time* and *Life,* essayizing ruminatively on the Beatles and drug culture for grown-ups who wanted to keep up. Goldman achieved his infamy, however, with his doorstop-size eighties biographies, *Elvis* and *The Lives of John Lennon*, which, in their exhaustively researched desire to expose the frailty and sociopathy of their subjects, revealed the even grubbier sociopathy of their author. The incandescent rage Goldman ignited in such rock-history curators as Jann Wenner was snuffed out in 1994 when Goldman died of a heart attack mid-flight en route to a TV appearance in London.

Green, Peter. Lead guitarist in the original, blues-based, all-English lineup of Fleetwood Mac. Revered in his day as a virtuoso on the order of Jimi Hendrix and Eric Clapton, Green abruptly withdrew from the spotlight in 1970 amid stories of SYD BARRETT–like drug intake and mental illness. After more than two decades of itinerant living, during which he sojourned on an Israeli kibbutz and sold off all his guitars, the once-lithe Green reemerged in the early 1990s as a rotund, Dickensian figure in a crocheted skullcap, playing Robert Johnson songs with a small blues combo. *Don't give me any of that "Rhiannon" crap; the real Mac is the sweet sound of* Peter Green *playing "Black Magic Woman."*

Gretsch. Georgia-based manufacturer of the only drum sets that matter to Snobs; the Jack Daniel's of musical-instrument manufacturers. (Lenny Kravitz alone once owned twenty Gretsch sets.) For the vast majority of his career, Charlie Watts has played a simple Gretsch four-piece (bass drum, snare, rack tom-tom, floor tom-tom) in emulation of cranky jazz deity Max Roach. *The last time I saw Elvin Jones at the Blue Note, he was attacking his* Gretsch *kit with the ferocity of a man a third his age.*

Hammond B3. Cumbersome, colonial-sideboard-resembling organ manufactured from the late thirties through the mid-seventies. Favored, despite its size and weight, by rock, soul, and blues musicians in the pre-synth era for its loudness and versatility, and by latter-day musicians for its "purity" of sound. Generally operated, since it lacks its own speaker, in conjunction with the equally unwieldy LESLIE tone cabinet. The Hammond B3 has been featured on everything from Bob Dylan's "Like a Rolling Stone" to the STAX recordings of Booker T. and the MGs to the PROG extravaganzas of Yes and Emerson, Lake & Palmer—though even Snobs are tripped up by the knowledge that it was actually a Hammond M102, and not a B3, that Procol Harum's Matthew Fisher played on in "A Whiter Shade of Pale."

Hammond, John. Natty, worldly producer and talent scout for Columbia Records whose chief claims to Snob cred—his discoveries of Bob Dylan, Aretha Franklin, and Bruce Springsteen—were merely the crowning achievements of a career that stretched back to the Jazz Age. Though he bore the bespoke, brush-cut appearance of an organization man, Hammond, who died in 1987, was a hipster who wrote for jazz rags and molded the careers of Billie Holiday, Benny Goodman, and Count Basie. Hammond's namesake son is a ROOTS-sensitive bluesman of some repute.

Hardy, Françoise. Achingly pretty French *chanteuse* of the sixties, known for her schoolgirlishly innocent pop songs—a sort of dreamy, uncorrupted counterpoint to the Gauloise-clouded, semen-stained Gallic sleaze-pop of SERGE GAINSBOURG—and for fending off the advances of such estimable suitors as Mick Jagger and Bob Dylan. Embraced today by EASY LISTENING devotees and people who read *Wallpaper* magazine, the still-beautiful Hardy has seen her Snob cred enhanced by nineties collaborations with Blur and Iggy Pop.

Hazlewood, Lee. Hard-drinkin', ultra-manly producer of Native American extraction who first made his name working with twangy guitar slinger Duane Eddy and went on to become the premier auteur of Rat Pack–offspring kitsch, writing and producing material for Dino, Desi and Billy, and, most notoriously, for Nancy Sinatra ("These Boots Are Made for Walkin'"). Following a 1973 solo debut candidly titled *Poet, Fool or Bum*, Hazlewood moved to Sweden and made lousy movies. Currently living in America again, where his oeuvre has been lovingly reissued by a small label owned by SONIC YOUTH drummer and confirmed Rock Snob Steve Shelley.

Lee Hazlewood

Hell, Richard. Charter member of the New York punk alliance, revered as a founding member of TELEVISION, coiner of the term "Blank Generation," and inventor of the ripped-clothing-and-electrocution-hair look that Malcolm McLaren filched for the Sex Pistols. Departing Television after a power struggle with his childhood friend and fellow adopter-of-a-silly-name Tom Verlaine (they grew up in Lexington, Kentucky, as Richard Meyers and Tom Miller and attended prep school together), Hell briefly enlisted with THE NEW YORK DOLLS refugee band the Heartbreakers before fronting his own combo, the Voidoids. Now a respected artperson who publishes novels and performs "poeokes" (hybrids of poetry readings and karaoke) at universities.

Hiatt, John. Affable ROOTS-rocker whose belated breakthrough in the late eighties anticipated the subsequent flourishing of ALT.COUNTRY and STEVE EARLE. A journeyman and an alcoholic who recorded several albums on different labels to little effect, Hiatt finally hit his stride when he cleaned up and recorded the hickory-smoked 1987 and 1988 albums *Bring the Family* and *Slow Turning*, the former of which supplied Bonnie Raitt with her comeback hit, "Thing Called Love." Though eclipsed in recent years by his lamentably less buoyant heirs, Hiatt has maintained visibility as a live attraction, and was the host of PBS's tolerable-music-television-for-Volvo-owners program, *Sessions at West 54th*, before it moved on to the Trio channel.

High Llamas, the. Inventive but underachieving English collective led by BRIAN WILSON– and BURT BACHARACH–worshipping musician-songwriter Sean O'Hagan. Way ahead of the curve, in 1993 O'Hagan anticipated the EASY-LISTENING craze with the High Llamas' debut, *Gideon Gaye*, a low-budget fusion of winsome melodies, lush strings, and close harmonies, and came even closer to the delicate grandeur of the Beach Boys' *Pet Sounds* with *Gideon Gaye*'s acclaimed follow-up, *Hawaii*. (In the late nineties, O'Hagan was briefly enlisted by the other Beach Boys to try to coax one last great album out of Wilson, but merely ended up frightening the ever reluctant auteur.) Unfortunately, subsequent High Llamas albums have suffered from metronomic monotony, though O'Hagan is in such high demand for his string arrangements (for such clients as Super Furry Animals, Stereolab, and the Doves), that he has been posited by Snobs as the new JACK NITZSCHE.

Hipgnosis. Obtuse design group responsible for Pink Floyd's landmark album covers (*Dark Side of the Moon*'s refracted light beam, *Animals*' pig flying over a smokestack, *Wish You Were Here*'s businessman aflame) as well as Led Zeppelin's *Houses of the Holy* cover (naked pink children

I

crawling up a primitive stone temple) and the record sleeves of various early-seventies PROG acts. Presided over by a pair of art-school fancy-pantses with the poncey names Storm Thorgerson and Aubrey Powell.

Ibanez Tube Screamer. Effects pedal widely popular with guitarists looking to coax a "fatter" sound from their transistor amplifiers. When first marketed in the seventies, the TS-808 model Tube Screamer cost around $30, and for years secondhand models were available for less, but demand from GARAGE PUNK retro rockers has now pushed the price toward $500. *I've tried lots of stomp boxes, but nothing beats my old, green* Ibanez Tube Screamer *for getting that sweet, chocolate-coated sustain.*

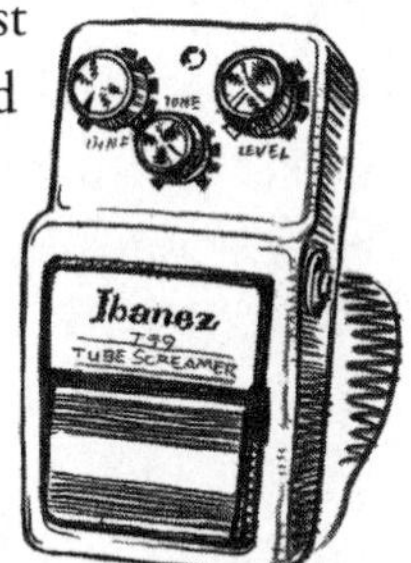

Ibanez Tube Screamer

-ica. Suffix employed by rock critics and musicians to bestow an air of vague futurism and internationalism upon mundane words (and often mundane music). Hence the genre electronica and the bands Republica, Elastica, and Panoptica. Björk almost called one of her albums *Domestica* before settling on the even more baffling *Vespertine.*

Ives, Charles. Willfully difficult New England–born composer (1874–1954) whose symphonic experiments in dissonance and microtonality (music that uses intervals of less than a semitone) have made him a crucial name-drop for academically inclined Snobs, as well as an important influence on such bridgers of rock and the avant-garde as VAN DYKE PARKS and GLENN BRANCA. Ives also held a full-time day job as an insurance executive. *Parks's* *audacious* Song Cycle *album is a riot of nickelodeon hurdy-gurdy and* Charles Ives *quotations.*

Jangle. Critic-beloved noun-adjective used to evoke sunny guitar pop; derived from Bob Dylan's allusion to the "jingle-jangle morning" in "Mr. Tambourine Man" and the chiming sound of the RICKENBACKER played by Dylan's foremost pop acolyte and songwriting beneficiary, the Byrds' Roger McGuinn. While most readily associated with the mid-sixties, the word "jangle" has also been applied to the precious pop of studenty English bands (such as the Smiths and Belle and Sebastian) and to L.A.'s flagrantly retro PAISLEY UNDERGROUND scene. *Nick Heyward's first solo record after leaving Haircut 100 is a lost masterpiece of* jangle-*pop.*

Jobriath. GLAM-rock oddity marketed as an openly gay rock star way back in 1973, long before gayness was a remotely market-friendly commodity. As if Jobriath's pedigree as a former *Hair* cast member and his overwrought, trash-operatic pop songs weren't questionable enough, his fate as a punching-bag-in-platforms was sealed when his record company mounted Times Square billboards and took out full-page ads in *Vogue* bearing his likeness. His second album stiffed in 1975, and Jobriath (né Bruce Campbell) died of AIDS-related illness in the early eighties, twenty years before posthumously scoring the ultimate Snob coup: his oeuvre reissued by RHINO Handmade, with liner notes by Morrissey.

Johns, Glyn and Andy. English brothers renowned as rock's premier recording engineers and producers from the late sixties through the seventies. Glyn, the elder, forsook a stillborn career as a pop singer to become Britrock's go-to engineer in its heyday, manning the boards for the Who, THE SMALL FACES, the Rolling Stones, Led Zeppelin, and, most controversially and Snob-worthily, for the Beatles during their fractious sessions for the album that was to have been called *Get Back*. (Glyn's raw, studio-verité version of the album, compiled when the Beatles themselves couldn't agree on what material should be included, and in what order, is still upheld as superior to both the Phil Spector desecration that became *Let It Be* and the 2003 McCartneyized remix known as *Let It Be . . . Naked*.) Andy, learning the ropes from Glyn, worked with Jimi Hendrix and Rod Stewart as well as the Stones and Led Zep, and is revered as the mic-placement genius behind John Bonham's tub-thumping showcase on *Led Zeppelin IV* (aka ZOSO), "When the Levee Breaks." Glyn's son Ethan is now a producer-musician-scenester in his own right, best known for his work with Ryan Adams.

Kent, Nick. Spindly legged rock critic of broken-down, opiated mien, often posited as an English analogue to LESTER BANGS. Kent was among the underground-press refugees who made the *New Musical Express* the essential rock read of the early seventies, specializing in rock's hardest of hard cases, writing mordant essays about the unravelings of BRIAN WILSON, SYD BARRETT, and ROKY ERICKSON while also touting every leather-clad, junked-up loser who would become SEMINAL to the punk revolution (Iggy Pop and THE NEW YORK DOLLS being his favorites). With his back-combed thatch and grafted-on leather trousers, Kent was himself something of a rock star in the pre-punk days, jamming with a then-unknown Chrissie Hynde and auditioning the nascent Sex Pistols, though, a few years later, he suffered a well-publicized chain-whipping at the hands of Sid Vicious.

THE ROCK SNOB BIBLIOGRAPHY

The Books That Every Snob Must Claim to Have Read

And the Ass Saw the Angel (1990), by Nick Cave. Australian crooner's Southern-gothic novel.

Back in the Days (2001), by Jamel Shabazz. Old-school hip-hop gets—!!!—coffee-table-book treatment.

Backstage Passes (1993), by Angie Bowie. Sloppy tell-all from bitchy glam-rock wife.

The Dark Stuff (2002), by Nick Kent, foreword by Iggy Pop. Compelling collection by cultish U.K. rock writer as notorious and romanticized as his drug-addled subjects.

Diary of a Rock 'n' Roll Star (1975), by Ian Hunter. Seventies tour diary by wry, self-aware Brit.

Dino (1992), by Nick Tosches. Powerhouse portrait of suave nihilism by hepcat author.

England's Dreaming (1992), by Jon Savage. Maturing punk rocker explains, with disarming lucidity, the Sex Pistols and postwar Britain in general.

Exploding (2001), by Stan Cornyn with Paul Scanlon. Ex–Warner Bros. exec chronicles his label's pre–corporate consolidation heyday.

Hammer of the Gods (1985), by Stephen Davies. Oddly touching story of yokel megastars on the loose; the source of a thousand scandalous Led Zep anecdotes, some of them true.

High Fidelity (1994), by Nick Hornby. The book every Snob wishes he'd written, and will never admit to having read.

Hit Men (1990), by Frederic Dannen. The industry . . . exposed!

Howling at the Moon (2004), by Walter Yetnikoff with David Ritz. CBS Records exec and villain of Dannen's *Hit Men* writes tell-all that's half mea culpa, half shameless celebration of *la vida coca*.

I'm With the Band (1987), by Pamela Des Barres. Amiable Cali-groupie memoir.

I Need More (1982), by Iggy Pop. Surprisingly erudite mini-memoir.

Lipstick Traces: A Secret History of the 20th Century (1989), by Greil Marcus. Brainy critic uses musings on Sex Pistols as launch pad for exploring every "ism" of the premillennial rebel culture.

Lobotomy: Surviving the Ramones (2000), by Dee Dee Ramone with Veronica Kofman and Legs McNeil. The literate one writes a credulity-straining but entertaining account of his clueless, history-making band.

Me, Alice (1976), by Alice Cooper and Steven Gaines. Out-of-print gem, first editions of which are worth up to $1,000.

Please Kill Me (1996), edited by Legs McNeil and Gillian McCain. Jovial oral history of American punk.

Psychotic Reactions and Carburetor Dung (1987), by Lester Bangs. Collected works of dead Snob-sanctified asshole critic, as presented by buddy Greil Marcus.

Revolution in the Head (1994), by Ian MacDonald. Britain's smartest but most humorless rock-crit head takes on the Beatles' recorded canon, session by session, riff by riff.

Rock Dreams (1973), by Nik Cohn and Guy Peelaert. Decadent visions of rock iconography, captioned with obituaries by a speed-freak superfan.

Stoned (2001) and *2Stoned* (2002), by Andrew Loog Oldham. Ex–Stones manager looks back with clarity gained through hindsight and rehab. And Scientology.

Up and Down with the Rolling Stones (1980), by Tony Sanchez. Keith's dealer reveals *some.*

Waiting for the Sun (1996), by Barney Hoskyns. Brit-in-L.A. takes on the whole of West Coast pop and comes through with anthropological epic.

Klaatu. Anonymous Canadian Beatles hommagistes who were briefly believed in 1977 to be the Beatles themselves, reunited under a pseudonym. In 1976 the Beatles' old label, Capitol, quietly released Klaatu's eponymous debut, a skillful evocation of the Fab Four's psychedelic phase. Whether through mischief or desperation, respected journalists, perhaps mindful that none of their "next Beatles" nominees had panned out (BADFINGER, Pilot, et al.), seized upon Klaatu as the stealthy return of the actual Beatles, kicking up a sirocco of wishful interpretation of the album's artwork and lyrics by dork fans. Once "outed" for who they really were, Klaatu faded back into obscurity, their gift to posterity being their song "Calling Occupants of Interplanetary Craft," which became a hit when covered by the Carpenters.

Knitting Factory, the. Lower Manhattan alternative-music club, instrumental in fomenting the eighties good-taste epidemic that saw experimental jazz and off-kilter pop get airings in unthreatening, coffeehouse-ish environments. Founded in 1987 on Houston Street by the genial music-world neophyte Michael Dorf, the Knitting Factory, with assists from such early regulars as HAL WILLNER, Wayne Horvitz, John Zorn, and BILL FRISELL, stumbled into its role as the locus of bespectacled, low-budget cool. Now a veritable brand name, the Knitting Factory has moved into larger digs in Tribeca, opened a Hollywood branch, and established an eclectic family of record labels that release everything from Don Byron's clarinet tootlings to PSYCH-pop to TRAD-JAZZ reissues.

Kraftwerk. Acutely German, acutely secretive inventors of "robot rock" (their preferred term), a highly mechanized dance-pop heavy on synthesizers, VOCODERs, and lyrics about robots, computers, trains, and bicycles. Founded in Düsseldorf in the late sixties by the KARLHEINZ STOCKHAUSEN–influenced art students Ralf Hütter and Florian Schneider, Kraftwerk effectively invented electronic pop music with their five albums released between 1974 and 1981, *Autobahn, Radioactivity, Trans-Europe Express, The Man Machine*, and *Computerworld*, all the while toying with Teutonic stereotypes by appearing in photographs as waxen, short-haired, emotionless mannequins. Hütter and Schneider have since become semi-recluses, infrequently releasing albums and playing live, though it's said that they beaver away at their Düsseldorf studio, KlingKlang, on a daily basis.

Kraftwerk

Krautrock. Blanket term for offbeat sixties and seventies music recorded by Germans, meaning everything from the robotic stylings of KRAFTWERK to the meandering soundscapes of Tangerine Dream to the starkly aggressive output of the dauntingly named bands Can (the most hippie-ish and least opaque), Neu! (whose members originally toiled in Kraftwerk), and Faust (who actually recorded a song called "Krautrock"). *New Order's early albums were flagrant in their borrowings from* Krautrock.

Kuti, Fela and Femi. Nigerian father-and-son exemplars of Afrobeat, a term Fela coined to describe his fusion of West African polyrhythms, jazz vamping, and seventies-style funk. The outsize, sax-tootin' Fela was a polygamist who had twenty-seven wives, boasted of Wilt Chamberlain levels of promiscuity, and was prone to performing in nothing but bikini briefs. He died of HIV-related illness in 1997, after a tumultuous life in which he sparred frequently with Nigeria's various military regimes. Fela's principled political stands, hypnotic music, and generally outré personality have made him, even in death, a cause célèbre of world-music Snobs, BRIAN ENO chief among them. His son Femi, who had been performing with Fela since his teens, carries on the Afrobeat legacy with the help of his (only) wife, who is actually named Funke.

La's, the. Short-lived Liverpool band unaccountably accorded legendary status by Snobs on the basis of one half-decent album of NEO-Merseybeat pop. Led by Lee Mavers, an obsessive who worked through several band lineups and producers in a vain attempt to capture some elusive LO-FI ideal in his bowl-cut-topped head, the La's finally saw their eponymous debut released against their leader's wishes in 1990, and scored a hit with the PLANGENT "There She Goes" (covered in 1997 by anemic Christian alt-poppers Sixpence None the Richer). Mavers subsequently retreated from public view, SYD BARRETT–style, amid rumors of mental illness, drug problems, and a trove of unreleased "masterpieces."

Last Poets, the. African-American spoken-word collective, often cited as precursors or even inventors of rap. Formed in the late sixties at the apex of the Black Power movement, the Poets, originally consisting of three actual poets and a drummer, electrified live audiences with their sonorous, cut-and-thrust indictments of both white and black America (for example, "Niggers Are Scared of Revolution") and recorded two SEMINAL proto-hip-hop albums, *The Last Poets* (1970) and *This Is Madness* (1971), that bore a heavy influence on such future tastemakers as Chuck D and Ice-T. Even the Poets, though, would fall prey to rock band–style factionalism, and, later, to arguments over which set of alumni has the right to tour under the original name. Currently, a version of the Last Poets featuring original member Abiodun Oyewole and later addition Umar Bin Hassan claims the title.

Laurel Canyon. Hilly Los Angeles neighborhood, located directly above Hollywood's Sunset Strip, that has come to represent a musical ideal and lifestyle ethos for the burgeoning legions of neo-hairy, seventies-AOR homagists. In the late sixties, much of L.A.'s new, hippie-pop aristocracy repaired to the woody, brownish Arts and Crafts houses that dot the canyon's twisty roads (the "very, very, very fine house" shared by Graham Nash and Joni Mitchell was on Lookout Mountain Avenue) and reinvented themselves for the coming decade as denimy, mildly countrified singer-songwriters. Though the scene quickly dissipated as its principals migrated westward to Malibu and northward to Santa Cruz and beyond, the "Laurel Canyon vibe" remains a touchstone for such blissed-out current acts as the Thorns (a quasi supergroup consisting of Matthew Sweet, Pete Droge, and Shawn Mullins) and the Thrills (a youthful quintet of California-obsessed Irishmen whose repertoire includes songs named "Big Sur" and "Don't Steal Our Sun").

Leslie, the. Hefty chunk of audio hardware originally designed as an amplifier for the HAMMOND B3 organ. The Leslie is distinguished by a high-range speaker horn that rotates atop its cabinet, lending a strange vibrato and distortion to the sounds that are processed through it. The Beatles forever expanded the utility of the Leslie when, eager for a dramatic effect in the final verse of "Tomorrow Never Knows," they broke into the circuitry of the cabinet and fed John Lennon's vocals through the speaker. Ever since, the Leslie has been put to similarly exotic uses—to make guitars sound like sitars on the Box Tops' 1967 hit "Cry Like a Baby," and to make Mick Jagger's vocals sound sinister on *Exile on Main Street*. More recently it has enhanced Portishead vocalist Beth Gibbons's atmospheric keening on a song entitled, in tribute, "Leslie."

Leslie

Lo-fi. Luddite recording aesthetic championed by contemporary artists who tend toward sparse, raw production and believe that older, analogue equipment produces a more "honest" or "organic" sound; or, more realistically, by artists too musically incompetent and undisciplined to record crafted, finished music. *At their best, Pavement combined Phi Beta Kappa smarts with an endearing* lo-fi *slipshodness.*

Lomax, Alan. Archivist, folklorist, and musicologist whose field recordings of indigenous performers in the American backwoods triggered the first wide-scale American appreciation of folk, blues, and traditional music—and, by extension, gave National Public Radio a reason to exist. Working in the thirties and forties under the aegises of CBS Radio and the Library of Congress, for which he was helping compile a folk-song archive, Lomax gave Leadbelly and Muddy Waters their first nationwide exposure. By the fifties, underwritten by the BBC, he'd moved on to Europe, where a similar harvesting of traditional songs precipitated a folk boom much like the one that Harry

Smith's *ANTHOLOGY OF AMERICAN FOLK MUSIC* set off in the United States. Hanging on 'til 2002, Lomax lived long enough to see his field recordings reconstituted by Moby as dance hits–cum–advertising jingles. *You can tell from the* O Brother, Where Art Thou? *soundtrack that the Coens are* Lomax *freaks.*

Louvin Brothers, the. Alabaman close-harmony duo of the fifties and sixties, consisting of siblings Ira (mandolin, high tenor) and Charlie (guitar, tenor). Preacherishly severe in appearance and possessed of a before-its-time gonzo sensibility (album titles include *Tragic Songs of Life* and *Satan Is Real*), the Louvins heavily influenced the slickness-averse pioneers of country rock—most especially GRAM PARSONS, for whom the volatile, alcoholic Ira, who died in a car crash in 1965, was an especially romantic figure of bottomed-out plaintiveness and self-immolation.

Louvin Brothers

Love. Baroque mid-sixties L.A. popsters led by Arthur Lee, a black hippie of prodigious talent and erratic discipline. Love's ability to combine such seemingly irreconcilable genres as psychedelia, West Coast sophisto-pop, mariachi, and GARAGE PUNK reached its apex with the band's 1967 album *Forever Changes.* Having spent much of the 1990s serving time in a California prison on an illegal-firearms possession charge, Lee, who often sports a luxuriant, Phil Spector–esque wig, has returned to the touring circuit to ecstatic response, particularly in Britain, where he was received by giddy Boomer MPs in the House of Commons, one of whom read a special proclamation declaring Love "the world's greatest rock band."

Macca. Journo-insiderist shorthand for Paul McCartney, often used with contempt or grudging affection. *I love* Abbey Road, *but "Maxwell's Silver Hammer" is a particularly atrocious* Macca *moment.*

Mardin, Arif. Turkish-born, elegantly mustachioed producer who, despite having been middle-aged since the seventies (he turned forty in '72), has proved shockingly canny and prescient in the dance and pop milieus—most notably when, charged with reviving the careers of the faded sixties boy-popsters the Bee Gees, he goaded Barry Gibb into singing in falsetto and writing R&B songs. Mardin was also the arranger of Aretha Franklin's "Respect," the producer of Chaka Khan's "I Feel For You," and, most recently, the overseer of Norah Jones's albums.

Marr, Johnny. Diminutive, seemingly mute guitarist who, as Morrissey's collaborator and foil in the Smiths in the eighties, constructed an impressively diverse array of musical backdrops for the singer's wounded plaints, from sprightly JANGLE-pop to spooked, *White Album*–ish minimalism to lavish, BACHARACH-redolent orchestralism. After the Smiths' demise in 1988, Marr proved so itinerant and noncommittal—playing with such acts as Talking Heads, Beck, and Pet Shop Boys, and doodling with synths in a hobby band with New Order's Bernard Sumner—that "pulling a Marr" became a Snob catchphrase for forsaking one's status as esteemed guitarist in a fine pop group for an uncertain, unfocused afterlife. Among those who've since pulled a Marr are the Stone Roses' John Squire, Suede's Bernard Butler, and Blur's Graham Coxon.

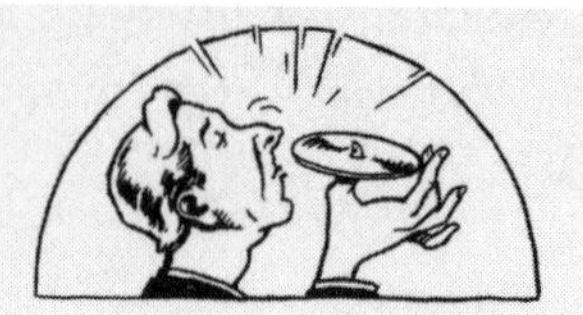

THE ROCK SNOB HALL OF SHAME

The Ten People Rock Snobs Are Required to Hate

Albert Goldman, critic and author. For swatting down the Lennon-as-peacenik mythology with his epic, misogynistic, bilious biography *The Lives of John Lennon*; for causing similar harm to the similarly dead Elvis in his Presley biography; for inducing feelings of guilt because some of his nasty reporting about Snob untouchables happens to be accurate.

Allen Klein, rapacious lawyer and business manager. For exacerbating tensions among the late-period Beatles, for his shoddy handling of the reissues of the Rolling Stones' early catalogue, for being generally scary and brutish long before the advent of gangsta rap.

Morris Levy, early rock mogul. For swindling rock music's black pioneers out of millions due them in royalties, for claiming songwriting credit on songs whose writing he had nothing to do with, for compelling John Lennon to record an abysmal record of

rock and roll covers as compensation for Lennon's having cribbed part of Chuck Berry's "You Can't Catch Me" for "Come Together."

Kurt Loder, MTV news anchor and former *Rolling Stone* scribe. For becoming the smirky Cronkite of the music-television era, for projecting an air of mild contempt for whatever subject matter he happened to be reporting on, for kissing Madonna's sculpted arse, for refusing to let go, for holding down the job that nine out of ten Snobs secretly feel should have been theirs.

Mike Love, Beach Boys vocalist. For dismissing the orchestral genius of cousin Brian Wilson's *Pet Sounds* as "ego music"; for continuing to trot out a bunch of anonymous paunchy guys in Hawaiian shirts as the Beach Boys; for having an adenoidal singing voice; for inexplicably baiting the Rolling Stones during his Rock and Roll Hall of Fame induction speech; for being the most tightly wound, un-Zen practitioner of transcendental meditation in history.

Jeff Lynne, former leader of Electric Light Orchestra. For placing himself on an artistic par with fellow Traveling Wilburys George Harrison, Bob Dylan, Roy Orbison, and Tom Petty; for having seventies bubble hair that resisted civilization's advance; for adding dated-sounding compressed drums to the "new" Beatles song "Free As a Bird"; for a Birmingham accent even more ludicrous than Ozzy's.

Paul McCartney, ex-Beatle. For being chipper to a near-sociopathic degree, for his relentless use of the thumbs-up gesture, for "Maxwell's Silver Hammer," for Wings, for recording with his wife but not in a cool Thurston Moore–Kim Gordon way, for *Give My Regards to Broad Street*, for not being John Lennon.

Colonel Tom Parker, manager of Elvis Presley. For neutering his client's primal talent, for frittering away Elvis's sixties in countless rocksploitation B-movies, for being neither a true colonel nor a true "Tom Parker" but a Dutchman named Dries Van Kuijk whose iffy immigration status precluded him from letting Elvis tour internationally, for turning Elvis into a docile and freakish Vegas cash cow.

Roger Waters, founder and bassist of Pink Floyd. For crabbily resisting reunions with the other three members of the group, for ungallantly (but accurately) explaining how prolific he was and how creatively deficient the others were, for making humorless solo albums that exuded dystopian zillionaire bitterness.

Jann Wenner, founder of *Rolling Stone*. For cozying up to both the rock establishment and the Jackie O.–Lee Radziwill set in the seventies; for selling out to Hollywood in the eighties; for preempting the "fat, dweeby groupie" taunts by becoming a lithe, stylish gay sybarite in the nineties; for turning his once-vital publication into a twenty-first-century lad mag.

Marshall stack. Monstrous amplification system designed to put out massive guitar sound from a proscenium, and, quite possibly, to make up for musicians' penile shortcomings. The Marshall stack is built from numerous rows of squat amplifiers sitting atop four-speaker cabinets, each black-fronted component bearing the scrolled "Marshall" logo. Designed in 1962 by Englishman Jim Marshall to provide rock guitarists with dirty tone and devilish torque, the stack has served the Rock God needs of everyone from Jimi Hendrix and Pete Townshend to Van Halen and Guns N' Roses. *In my fantasies I am Slash, a screaming crowd before me and a* Marshall stack *behind me.*

Master Musicians of Jajouka, the. More respected than enjoyed Moroccan collective whose members play the ancient devotional music of the peoples of the Er Rif Mountains, near Tangier. Though their wailing horns and pipes and polyrhythmic drumming often make for mesmerizing listening, the Master Musicians, who were first given Western exposure by such druggie adventurers as William S. Burroughs and the Rolling Stones' Brian Jones, are most readily revered by killjoy World Music Snobs (chief among them was the late *New York Times* critic Robert Palmer), who view their work as the musical equivalent of oat bran, to be dutifully taken in as nourishment rather than as a sensual experience. *I can't be bothered with rock music anymore; all I listen to is Miles Davis's* Nefertiti *and the* Master Musicians of Jajouka.

Math rock. Ridiculous micro-trend whose indie-rock practitioners abruptly shift time signatures from one bar to the next (from, say, four-four to six-eight to seven-four, hence the "math" designation) and pride themselves on their "tight" playing. Akin to the sound of seventies and eighties wank-rock specialists Rush, with more pronounced punk overtones and less hair.

Mayall, John. Lean, bearded English blues guitarist of slightly pre-rock vintage (born in 1933) whose sixties band, John Mayall's Bluesbreakers, served as a finishing school for Britain's future blues-rock and seventies AOR elite, among them Eric Clapton, who'd fled the pop constraints of the Yardbirds; Jack Bruce, with whom Clapton would form Cream; Mick Taylor, later of the Rolling Stones; and the future Fleetwood Mac's PETER GREEN, Mick Fleetwood, and John McVie. Though his blues purism caused him some lean times in the airbrushed seventies, during which he relocated to LAUREL CANYON, Mayall is now recognized as a SEMINAL figure and, in his seventies, is a reliable live draw with his current lineup of Bluesbreakers.

MC5, the. Wild-eyed, butt-ugly rhetoricians who emerged from Detroit's White Panther enclave in 1969 to debut with the insurrectionary live album *Kick Out the Jams* (whose title song amended this command with the word "motherfuckers!"). *Kick Out the Jams* and its follow-up, *Back in the USA*, stood in bracing contrast to the hippie noodlings offered up by other bands of the era; dropping the MC5's name—and that of its decadent Detroit neighbors THE STOOGES—was positively de rigueur for British punk's class of 1977. In America, MC5 chic reared its head again with the advent of the White Stripes–anchored "new Detroit scene."

McGee, Alan. Knob-headed, grandiose Scotsman best known for founding Creation Records, independent home to ineffectual guitar-pop dreamers. After Sony bought into his company, McGee scored his sole legitimate success by signing Oasis—the band that symbolized Britpop at its mid-nineties, cocaine-fueled apogee and gave the headline-hungry McGee direct access to Tony Blair. The consequent hubris led McGee to believe he could make stars of no-hope acts and revive the careers of his early-eighties idols, among them Kevin Rowland of DEXYS MIDNIGHT RUNNERS and Nick Heyward of Haircut 100. After Creation fizzled in 1999, McGee founded the even more precious Poptones label, which specialized in new, fringe-haired POWER-POP bands and "from the vaults" excavations of forgotten works by such sixties-pop Snob favorites as CURT BOETTCHER.

McTell, Blind Willie. Georgia bluesman whose legend has been burnished by the fact that relatively little is known about him (he died shortly before the early-sixties folk-blues revival) and the Snob-pleasing cadence of his name. With his quavery, androgynous voice and an especially difficult back catalogue to navigate—he recorded sporadically on several different labels, under several different names, including Georgia Bill, Pig 'n Whistle Red, and Barrelhouse Sammy—McTell has proven irresistible to Heritage Snobs, all the more so since the 1991 release of Bob Dylan's Bootleg Series, volumes 1 to 3, which included a tribute song that declared, "Nobody can sing the blues like Blind Willie McTell." *I can't be bothered with rock music anymore; all I listen to is Juke Boy Bonner and* Blind Willie McTell.

Meek, Joe. Ill-starred producer of bizarro early-sixties Anglo-pop singles. Working out of a studio in his bedroom in North London, he sprayed stardust upon pop aspirants of no discernible talent, using primitive electronics and his own ingenuity to fashion clangorous hits for such nonentities as the Honeycombs ("Have I the Right") and the Tornados ("Telstar"). A gay, British counterpart to Phil Spector, Meek, too, found himself marginalized when the Beatles turned musicians into "artists," and died by his own hand in 1967, in a murder-suicide that also claimed his landlady.

Joe Meek

Mellotron. Primitive sixties synthesizer whose keys, when pressed, activate prerecorded tape loops; used to famous effect in the opening bars of "Strawberry Fields Forever." Vintage mellotrons are now purchased at great cost (usually in the low five figures) by retro rockers angling to sound Beatles-esque. *Let's put some* mellotron *over the fade-out to make it really* Revolver*ish.*

Meters, the. Almost unlistenably funky New Orleans band, led by Art Neville of the Neville Brothers. Ever since their formation in the late sixties, the Meters have been a connoisseur's buy rather than a mainstream attraction, mainly because of the algorithmic complexity of their music. Nevertheless, white boys Paul McCartney and Robert Palmer were sufficiently undeterred to record with them in the seventies, and Snob arbiter Damon Albarn of Blur showboats his Meters fandom. The melanin-deficient Snob monthly *MOJO* has decreed the Meters "probably the funkiest band of all time."

MIDI. Abbreviation for Musical Instrument Digital Interface, a communications protocol that allows a central electronic device, usually a keyboard or computer, to interact with other MIDI-compatible devices, enabling one person to command several instruments at once—and to tweak, twiddle, and layer every last note and beat of a composition to one's heart's content. MIDI, which was developed by a consortium of musical-instrument manufacturers (among them Yamaha, Roland, and Korg), was viewed warily by many purists when it was introduced in 1983, but is now used by nearly all rock musicians save the White Stripes. *With all my* MIDI *sequencers and interfaces, I can perform* The Wall *without David, Rick, or Nick, God help them.*

Midnight Special, the. Lightweight, less threatening counterpoint to *DON KIRSHNER'S ROCK CONCERT*, aired after *The Tonight Show* on Friday nights in the seventies. Though marred by network concessions to schlock mores, such as grating interjections from announcer Wolfman Jack and the occasional appearance of an atrocious BUBBLEGUM act like Bo Donaldson and the Heywoods, *The Midnight Special* nevertheless offered American viewers a chance to see David Bowie and MICK RONSON at the height of their *Ziggy Stardust* androgyny and performances by Alice Cooper, Rod Stewart, and Aerosmith that now delight Archivalist Snobs on video.

Mojo. English magazine offering an exuberant, high-production-values take on Rock Snobbery; *the* compulsory Snob read since its founding in 1992. A typical issue offers a reverent interview with a crinkly rocker of sixties vintage, a couple of multipage, photo-laden articles on suitably obscurist topics (such as the Doug Yule–era Velvet Underground or the triumphal years of English blues plodders Free), and some sort of article on NICK DRAKE.

Monks, the. Entrancingly strange mid-sixties beat combo composed of five American GIs who remained in Germany beyond their tour of duty. True to their collective name, these musical Colonel Kurtzes wore habits, sandals, and Friar Tuck tonsures. Even stranger was their music, a nihilistic, ramshackle assault that unwittingly foreshadowed punk rock by a decade. A one-off proposition if ever there was one, the Monks enjoyed a surprising revival in 1999, when their lone album was reissued to acclaim and they embarked on a reunion tour, scalps re-tonsured and everything.

Monterey Pop. Shorthand for the Monterey International Pop Festival, held over two days in June of 1967 in the coastal Californian town and viewed as a nexus between the tidy, besuited era of pop and the druggy, nasty, hairy era of rock. Organized by LOU ADLER and JOHN PHILLIPS as a way of uniting rock music's shiny L.A. acts (the Mamas and the Papas, the Byrds) and the emerging San Francisco hippie acts (the Grateful Dead, the Jefferson Airplane, Big Brother and the Holding Company), the Monterey Pop festival also functioned as a feeding ground for major-label sharks itching to co-opt the "youth scene" by signing bands to lucrative contracts—thus impelling Snobs to rue Monterey as the beginning of the corrupt, ruthless era of big-time corporate rock (as opposed to the preceding corrupt, ruthless era of small-time Mob-run pop). The festival was also the occasion for the indelible moment in which Jimi Hendrix set fire to his guitar while playing THE TROGGS's "Wild Thing."

Moog. Squelching OLD-SCHOOL synthesizer invented in 1965 and first popularized by WALTER CARLOS's bachelor-pad suite *Switched-On Bach.* The prodigiously corded instrument (and its Austin Powers–sounding offspring, the MiniMoog) went on to become a staple of PROG and KRAUTROCK. Today, the Moog is fetishized by vintage-instrument enthusiasts such as Beck, as well as dance-music impresarios like Fatboy Slim, who remixed a track on a kitschy *Best of Moog* compilation.

Morricone, Ennio. Prolific Italian composer of music for films, most notably his old schoolmate Sergio Leone's famous spaghetti Westerns *A Fistful of Dollars, Once Upon a Time in the West*, and *The Good, the Bad and the Ugly*. Though Morricone continues to churn out scores for both Hollywood and European movies, it's his atmospheric 1960s work that has made him the patron saint of such upscale-Snob mood-musicians as Goldfrapp (whose icy-cool chanteuse, Allison Goldfrapp, thanked "Ennio" in her first album's sleeve notes).

Muscle Shoals Rhythm Section. Crack four-piece of white Alabama boys (Barry Beckett, keyboards; Jimmy Johnson, guitar; Roger Hawkins, drums; David Hood, bass) responsible for underpinning such soul classics as Aretha Franklin's "I Never Loved a Man (The Way I Love You)" and Wilson Pickett's "Mustang Sally." In 1969 the group opened its own Muscle Shoals Sound Studios, which in subsequent years became a pilgrimage destination for such swamp-vibe seekers as the Rolling Stones, Paul Simon, and Bob Dylan. Snobs like to refer to the Muscle Shoals four as the Swampers, the insiderist nickname assigned them by beardy WRECKING CREW stalwart Leon Russell.

My Bloody Valentine. Erstwhile great white hypes of British guitar rock, heralded in the mid-eighties as a groundbreaking amalgam of noise, melody, and psychedelia—despite offering a rather ordinary if occasionally pleasing indie drone-pop sound. The band's leader, Kevin Shields, achieved a degree of infamy for nearly bankrupting ALAN McGEE's Creation Records by taking two years to record My Bloody Valentine's dud 1991 album, *Loveless*, and then "buggering off" with a million more pounds in advances from three different record companies. These companies received no return for their investments, but the reclusive Shields finally resurfaced in the twenty-first century—complete with prosperous waistline—as a touring guitarist with the band Primal Scream and the composer of the soundtrack for Sofia Coppola's *Lost in Translation*.

Nanker Phelge. Esoteric pseudonym that appears throughout the early Rolling Stones publishing catalogue, usually to denote group-written compositions. "Phelge" was the Dickensian, onomatopoeic surname of an unhygienic roommate who shared a Chelsea flat with Mick Jagger, Keith Richards, and Brian Jones in the early sixties, while "nanker" was an onomatopoeic verb invented by the group to describe the crude mannerisms and wretched physiognomy of London's underclass.

Neil, Fred. Ringleted, mild-mannered folkie and early Dylan acolyte (1936–2001) best known for his anti-urban plaint "Everybody's Talkin'," which was sung by HARRY NILSSON on the *Midnight Cowboy* soundtrack. Painfully shy and empathetic, Neil identified more with dolphins than with humans (his elegiac song "Dolphins" was covered by TIM BUCKLEY), and lived out his final decades in blissful anonymity in the Florida Keys, paining Rock Snobs by refusing to record new music.

Neo-. Generous rock-critic term for "refried," usually used to elevate knowing hommagistes above the station of mere tribute bands. *The Strokes'* Room on Fire *is a delightful platter of* neo*–New York punk.*

Nesmith, Michael. Singer-songwriter whose civilian standing as the wool-hatted, least-reunion-inclined member of the Monkees is trumped in Snob circles by his standing as a progenitor of country rock. Nesmith recovered from Monkeedom by releasing three GRAM PARSONS–worthy albums with his First National Band in 1970–71, *Magnetic South, Loose Salute*, and *Nevada Fighter*, all of which sold poorly but hold up surprisingly well. Also known for having "invented" MTV, by virtue of having sold his concept for an all-music television program called *Pop Clips* to Time Warner (which developed his idea into a network), and for being the heir to the Liquid Paper fortune.

Neumann U47. German-made microphone beloved for the clarity and warmth of its sound, despite its having been developed from a model used by Hitler at Nazi rallies. Frank Sinatra would not sing a word without his U47, which he called a "Telly" because the microphone was marketed by Telefunken in the United States. The Beatles used the slightly more advanced U48 on *Abbey Road*. Although a modernized version of the U47 is widely available, studio-equipment Snobs will always use the vintage model, with its reputedly magical VF-14 valve.

Neumann U47

Neve. British manufacturer of high-end, Snob-fetishized mixing consoles. While purists such as the producer Rick Rubin love to twiddle the faders of the vintage, analogue

Neve 8048 desk, and technophiles of the JEFF "SKUNK" BAXTER ilk hail Neve's groundbreaking Capricorn digital consoles, the company's biggest paradigm shifter was its Necam automated mixing system, introduced in the late seventies, which allowed producers to save onto floppy disk every nuance of complicated multitrack mixes—something of a mixed blessing in that hermetic, studio-perfectionist era, during which Steely Dan's Donald Fagen put exasperated engineers at Los Angeles' Village Recorder studios through almost 300 Necam mixes of one song during the *Gaucho* sessions. Fagen finally settled on mix No. 274, though he returned to the studio a few days later to fix a single bass note in the second bar.

New York Dolls, the. Ill-starred, shambolic, drag-dressing GLAM-rock band that held the fort for New York sleaze rock during the early-seventies interregnum between the Velvet Underground and punk. Though they flamed out even faster than fellow proto-punk degenerates THE STOOGES, disintegrating after just two albums (the second of which was aptly named *Too Much Too Soon*), the Dolls have posthumously evolved into a brand name for depravity chic, their logo emblazoning clingy stretch T's for sale in adorable little boutiques on the very same Lower East Side blocks where haystack-haired guitarist Johnny Thunders scored junk. Singer David Johansen eventually graduated to the eighties good-taste epidemic as crooner Buster Poindexter, while Thunders and drummer Jerry Nolan, a fellow junkie, formed the "legendary" punk band the Heartbreakers (briefly abetted by RICHARD HELL) before dying of drug-related causes in 1991 and 1992, respectively.

Nico. Compellingly doomed German-born model (née Christa Päffgen) whose severe cheekbones, six-foot height, and natural state of nihilistic ennui inspired Andy Warhol to graft her to the Velvet Underground as a "chanteuse." Though she only sang "three lonely songs," as she put it, on the Velvets' debut album, her thudding, off-key readings were nonetheless winning in a spooky, Weimarish way, and the two melancholy albums she recorded after leaving the group, *Chelsea Girl* and *The Marble Index*, became Snob causes célèbres even before Nico's suitably tragic death in a bicycle accident in 1988. Often twinned with MARIANNE FAITHFULL in the annals of frosty, rock-damaged beauties, Nico, too, was hooked on heroin, and claimed a roster of conquests that overlaps with and arguably bests Faithfull's, its number including Jim Morrison, Bob Dylan, Jackson Browne, Brian Jones, Alain Delon, Iggy Pop, John Cale, and Lou Reed.

Nilsson, Harry. Brooklyn-born, powerfully piped singer-songwriter equally famous for well-realized retro-pop albums such as *Nilsson Schmilsson* (1971) and for being John Lennon's drinking buddy/partner in crime during the latter's *Lost Weekend* period in Los Angeles. Though his adept melding of Tin Pan Alley and *Sgt. Pepper* idioms suggested an artist of limitless possibility in the late sixties and early seventies, his increasingly sozzled state put him into a mid-seventies artistic decline from which he never recovered. (His tipple of choice was the brandy Alexander, which the admiring Lennon referred to as a "milkshake.") Since his 1994 death, however, Nilsson has acquired significant hipster cachet, with his oeuvre lavishly repackaged by BMG and his song "One," as sung by Aimee Mann, used prominently over the credits of P. T. Anderson's 1999 epic *Magnolia*.

Harry Nilsson

THE ROCK SNOB HALL OF FAME

The Unimpeachable Torchbearers of True Rock Snobbery

Beastie Boys, ageless hip-hop collective. For their impeccable curation of the seventies funk revival, for their diligent exhumation of obscure soul and dub sides, for their namechecks of Lee Dorsey and Lee "Scratch" Perry, for releasing Sean Lennon's solo LP on their Grand Royal label, for unleashing the "mullet" phenomenon.

Jack Black, cuddly, kinetic comic. For predicating the better part of a film career on playing a hyper-ventilating Rock Snob, for actually *being* a hyper-ventilating Rock Snob, for knowingly targeting prog rock as a loamy mother lode of rock satire, for possessing the "chops" of a true prog believer.

David Chase, creator of *The Sopranos.* For always nailing his end-credits song choice with laserlike Snob precision (Elvis Costello's "Complicated Shadows,"

the Kinks' "I'm Not Like Everybody Else," Bobby Darin's "If I Were a Carpenter," etc.), for basing the character Hesh Rabkin on Snob bête noire Morris Levy, for the audaciously show-offy "Every Breath You Take"–"Theme from *Peter Gunn*" remix, for employing real musical figures (Steven Van Zandt, David Lee Roth, Frankie Valli) as found-object actors.

Elvis Costello, singer-songwriter. For covering Dusty Springfield tunes during the New Wave wars; for producing the Specials and the Pogues; for casually namechecking Stravinsky and Destiny's Child in the same interview; for being UCLA's artist in residence; for collaborating with Burt Bacharach, Elvis Presley's backing musicians, and the Swedish mezzo-soprano Anne Sofie von Otter; for knowing more about every Snob angle than you ever will.

Cameron Crowe, *Rolling Stone* boy-journo turned movie director. For convincingly selling the improbable notion that you can win the heart of a cute outsider-girl with Peter Gabriel's music *Say Anything*); for using the obscure, trippy post-commercial Beach Boys song "Feel Flows" over the closing credits of *Almost Famous*; for using the obscure, post-commercial Monkees song "The Porpoise Song" during a freakout scene in *Vanilla Sky*.

John Cusack, actor. For playing the Snob Romantic to Jack Black's Snob Jester, for absorbing the lessons of faded Snob mentor John Hughes and infusing his films with choice tunes for outsiderish dudes (for example, the Clash's "Rudie Can't Fail" and the Violent Femmes' "Blister in the Sun" in *Grosse Pointe Blank*), for bringing to the screen Nick Hornby's Snob-centric *High Fidelity*.

Nick Hornby, novelist. For compiling the first comprehensive anthropological study of the Rock Snob (in the form of his novel *High Fidelity*), for transmuting *High Fidelity*'s success into a second career as a genial Snob essayist, for reclassifying mix tapes and "best-of" lists from time-wasting wankery into trenchant forms of self-expression.

Lenny Kaye, riffmeister-archivist. For compiling the *Nuggets* anthology of garage rock in the early seventies and being among the first to recognize the durability of shoddy, Brit-imitative 45s; for cofounding the Patti Smith Group; for cementing his status as leather-trewed prime mover by teaching an American Studies course on rock music at Rutgers University.

Courtney Love, singer-actress-tragedy. For being an indie-rock know-it-all; for fulfilling the fantasy of every torn-stocking goth fat-girl who hung out at the British-import record shop in 1983; for presciently embracing Laurel Canyonism and Fleetwood Mac revivalism on her attempted sellout album, *Celebrity Skin*; for keeping the flame alive with drug allegations, street hassles, and interviews that namecheck Jim Steinman *and* Gang of Four.

Morrissey, singer-lyricist-curmudgeon. For publishing a New York Dolls fanzine before the world caught on, for reuniting the dessicated remains of the Dolls for a 2004 U.K. festival, for being a scarily obsessive champion of beautiful losers like Sparks and Jobriath, for dismissively referring to Britney Spears as "Broccoli Spears."

Martin Scorsese, director. For pioneering the use of jukebox pop as a cine-violence lubricant (for example, the pool-hall fight to the strains of the Marvelettes' "Please Mr. Postman" in *Mean Streets*); for the devastating deployment of Harry Nilsson's "Jump Into the Fire" at the climax of *GoodFellas*; for not only filming the Band's swansong, *The Last Waltz,* but bunking down with Robbie Robertson for their shared "Lost Weekend" period.

Nitzsche, Jack. Runty, cantankerous Phil Spector protégé who started out as a session pianist but quickly graduated to status as rock's A-list arranger, working with Neil Young, the Rolling Stones, and TIM BUCKLEY. Though his ambitions as a recording artist were extinguished with the poor sales of his 1972 opus *St. Giles Cripplegate*, he gained new renown as a soundtrack composer; movies as diverse as *Performance, One Flew Over the Cuckoo's Nest*, and *An Officer and a Gentleman* bear his spectral imprimatur. *Check out that awesome* Nitzsche *arrangement on Springfield's "Expecting to Fly."*

Northern Soul. Fervent, inexplicable English musical cult predicated on the fetishization of post-Motown regional soul labels and the deification of minor U.S. soul acts such as the Tams, Major Lance, and Gloria Jones. At its peak in the early to mid-1970s, Northern Soul, as popularized in Northern England clubs like the Wigan Casino and Blackpool's Mecca, had the power to propel singles of improbable provenance into the U.K. Top 20 and to make its working-class adherents subscribe to an unforgiving, speed-fueled lifestyle of stylized dervish dancing and unflattering wide trousers. A diminished version of the scene persists to this day.

Norwegian death metal. Ultra-Gothic subgenre of heavy metal whose Scandinavian adherents embrance the occultist and medievalist motifs (pentagrams, capes, inverted crosses, etc.) that their English and American metal forebears grew sick of around 1978. Though an escapist kick for American hobbyists (Jack Osbourne was seen on TV blasting Norwegian death metal at his neighbors), the music is more authentically threatening in its homeland, where one risibly named death-metal star, Count Grishnackh, is serving time for the 1993 murder of another, Euronymous.

No Wave. Droll late-seventies alliance between artpersons living on New York's Lower East Side and the fraying CBGB–Max's Kansas City punk movement. A lodestar for many of today's young GARAGE PUNK bands, No Wave was capable of being screechingly dissonant and David Byrne–ishly arch at the same time (GLENN BRANCA was in a No Wave act called Theoretical Girls) and sometimes veered into free jazz and/or sparse funk. (Grandmaster Flash lifted the "White Lines" bass line from the song "Cavern," by the No Wave stalwarts Liquid Liquid.) In 1978, BRIAN ENO put No Wave on the map with his SEMINAL *No New York* compilation LP, which featured such once and future Downtown scenesters as James Chance, Arto Lindsay (then with the group DNA), and Lydia Lunch (then with Teenage Jesus and the Jerks).

Nudie's Rodeo Tailors. Hollywood-based clothing shop specializing in gaudy, rhinestone-studded Western wear. Though Kiev-born Nudka Cohn had been in business since 1947 (catering originally to movie-Western actors and such country stars as Hank Williams and PORTER WAGONER), Nudie's acquired Snob significance only in the late sixties, when GRAM PARSONS outfitted himself and his fellow Flying Burrito Brothers in custom Nudie suits with psychedelic motifs (marijuana leaves, puffy clouds, etc.). The Nudie look has since been "rocked" by Beck and, during his *Monster*-era visual-identity crisis, R.E.M.'s Mike Mills.

Nuggets. Landmark anthology LP of obscurish sixties "punk" singles by one-hit-wonder garage bands, compiled in 1972 by Lenny Kaye, a scrawny, prototypical rock nerd who would shortly thereafter be a prime mover in the seventies punk movement as the guitarist for the Patti Smith Group. *Early Nirvana combined Beatles-esque songcraft with* Nuggets*-y abandon.*

Nyro, Laura. Bronx-born progenitor of soulful *Rhoda*-rock. The precocious Nyro released her debut album in 1966 at the age of nineteen, and shortly thereafter saw the Fifth Dimension and Barbra Streisand score hits with her free-swinging compositions "Wedding Bell Blues" and "Stoney End," respectively. Snapped up by aspiring agent David Geffen, she signed a $4 million contract with Columbia Records—putting both herself and Geffen in the big leagues—and released two SEMINAL albums, *Eli and the Thirteenth Confession* and *New York Tendaberry*, before growing fed up with the music industry and the limitations it placed on her free spirit and eccentric habits. (She demanded, for instance, that one of her albums be pressed on perfume-infused vinyl, and named her publishing company Tuna Fish Music, after her daily lunch choice.) At the age of twenty-four, Nyro moved from Manhattan to New England, and flitted in and out of retirement until her death in 1997.

Laura Nyro

Oberheim. Manufacturer of acutely eighties musical equipment now valued, like the FAIRLIGHT synthesizer, for its period-specific sound. Oberheim's DMX drum machine produced the thick, unnuanced *thwack* that underpins both the OLD-SCHOOL hits of Run-DMC and the retro-disco workouts of the Parisian dance duo Daft Punk,

O

while the company's similarly revived OB8 keyboard became a visual staple when Eddie Van Halen played it in the video for his group's song "Jump."

Oldham, Andrew Loog. Dizzyingly brazen and Soho-fabulous manager of the Rolling Stones in their early days. The self-inventedly posh son of an English-Jewish widow whose American-soldier boyfriend died before Andrew was born, Oldham was still in his teens when he hustled the Stones into letting him handle them, making them famous by sheer force of personality—concocting their bad-boy image with his "Would you let your daughter date a Stone?" campaign, forcing uncute sixth member Ian Stewart out of the official lineup, and acting as the behavioral template for Mick Jagger, who appropriated Oldham's camp, preening persona wholesale. Oldham also manufactured MARIANNE FAITHFULL's stardom, famously proclaiming her to be "an angel with big tits." After a long wilderness period as a bearded, djellaba'd drug casualty, Oldham cleaned up via Scientology and returned to the fray in the new millennium with two of the best, most candid memoirs in the Snob canon, *Stoned* and *2Stoned.*

Old school. Sometimes spelled *old skool.* Originally a discursively valid term that functioned as the hip-hop equivalent of the word "classic" in rock, denoting a performer or phenomenon from an earlier era still held in high regard today: *Eric B and Rakim are my* old-school *faves.* But more recently the term has transmogrified into a despicable phraseological device employed by honkies angling for hipster credibility: *I'm much more into* old-school *Banana Republic, back when it was all safari-wear.*

O'Rourke, Jim. Chicago-bred, impeccably credentialed titan of difficult but rewarding rock. Though an unassuming, frumpy figure in his drab thrift-shop wear, O'Rourke is held in awe by Rock Snobbery's obtuse wing for his flourishing quadruple-threat career as a solo artist, producer/mixer (Wilco, Tortoise, Stereolab, Smog), part-time member of various avant-rock collectives (Gastr del Sol, Fenno'berg, the Red Krayola), and, as of 2001, full-fledged member of the ageless upscale noiseniks SONIC YOUTH. Further impresses Film Snobs by naming his albums after difficult but rewarding Nicolas Roeg movies (*Insignificance, Bad Timing*).

Otis, Shuggie. Troubled former funk prodigy renowned for having turned down the opportunity to replace Mick Taylor in the Rolling Stones. The son of revered Los Angeles R&B bandleader Johnny Otis, Shuggie, a prodigiously Afro'd multi-instrumentalist, took a then unheard-of three years to record his third album, *Inspiration Information*, in the early seventies—so infuriating his label, Epic, that it dropped him, effectively extinguishing his career. The album, an amalgam of soul, funk, and electro-pop that simultaneously recalled Sly Stone and anticipated Prince, sank without a trace upon its 1974 release, but was rereleased in 2001 to orgiastic Snob response (with a sleeve endorsement from the HIGH LLAMAS' Sean O'Hagan), precipitating the mentally fragile Otis's shaky reentry into public life, à la BRIAN WILSON, PETER GREEN, and LOVE's Arthur Lee.

Shuggie Otis

Outsider music. Broad term for any music played or recorded by nonprofessional musicians or, in some cases, by professional musicians who ought to consider another line of work. Among outsider music's causes célèbres are the Shaggs, the laughably incompetent trio of working-class New Hampshire sisters whose deluded father corraled them into recording an album in 1969 (which Frank Zappa pronounced "better than the Beatles"), and the seventies Canadian schoolchildren heard on the exuberantly received *Langley Schools Music Project* album, whose hippie teacher coaxed oddly affecting renditions of then contemporary soft-rock hits from them. Outsider music's Dr. Demento–ish doyen, Irwin Chusid (who also happens to be the man who repopularized the Mexican EASY-LISTENING godhead Esquivel), hosts a weekly radio program, entitled "Incorrect Music," that straddles a difficult line between affection and amused contempt for its showcased performers, not a few of whom are mentally ill.

Paisley Underground. Pleasant-enough but recklessly overrated NEO-psychedelic JANGLE-pop movement of the eighties, centered around the Southern California bands the Dream Syndicate, the Long Ryders, the Bangles, the Three O'Clock, Green on Red, and Rain Parade. By virtue of having been a genuinely cohesive scene (the bands shared bills and members) and having eschewed the abominable synth-production mores of the day, the Paisley Underground received favorable attention from the music press and college radio, but its fey Anglophilia (the Bangles were originally called Colours), tidied-up King's Road wardrobes (lots of brocade vests and top-button buttoning), and merely B-plus musical output consigned it to extinction at decade's end.

Parks, Van Dyke. Campy, Southern-born, half-pint composer-lyricist best known for being tapped by BRIAN

WILSON to write the words to the Beach Boys' aborted *Smile* album. Though Parks's bizarre, Joycean, free-associative lyrics served him well on his own albums (such as the Rock Snob orchestral-pop favorites *Song Cycle* [1968] and *Discover America* [1972]), his baroque tendencies (including the deathless line "Columnated ruins domino" in the song "Surf's Up") alienated the other Beach Boys and exacerbated tensions within the group. Parks and Wilson reteamed on the 1995 album *Orange Crate Art*, and again on their 2004 effort to reconstitute *Smile*.

Parsons, Gram. Southern, Harvard-educated, trustafarian pretty-boy who invented country rock by bringing his high-lonesome tastes to bear on his one album as a Byrd (1968's *Sweetheart of the Rodeo*, considered the first country-rock LP). Parsons and fellow Byrd Chris Hillman went on to form the Flying Burrito Brothers. A hard-livin' soul who favored tightfitting NUDIE suits custom-decorated with pictures of naked girls and marijuana leaves, he greatly impressed Mick Jagger and Keith Richards (inspiring them to write "Wild Horses"), and recorded two Rock Snob–ratified solo albums, *GP* and *Grievous Angel*, before dying of a morphine-and-alcohol overdose in a motel in Joshua Tree, California, in 1973 at the age of twenty-six.

Gram Parsons

Partch, Harry. Crusty, iconoclastic composer (1901–1974) best known for inventing his own instruments—such as the Bloboy, the Chromelodeon, the Kithara, the Zymo-xyl, and the Marimba Eroica—on which one could play his compositions, which exceeded even CHARLES IVES's in microtonal experimentation. (Partch's octaves had forty-three tones in them.) With his madman's demeanor, background as a Depression-era hobo, junk-shop aesthetic (the Zymoxyl was made in part from liquor bottles and hubcaps), and general wooziness of sound, Partch was a clear antecedent to both Tom Waits and the OUTSIDER MUSIC movement. *Tomorrow evening, folks, we have the Kronos Quartet performing music by* Harry Partch, *so keep it right here at listener-supported WNYC . . .*

Pedal steel. Tricky-to-play but ROOTSily atmospheric string instrument, essentially a guitar neck (or two) mounted on a small table and played sitting down, guiding a steel bar up and down the fretboard while operating a series of foot pedals and knee levers. Long a staple of Hawaiian music and straight country, the pedal steel acquired rock credibility with the Flying Burrito Brothers' addition of pedal-steel whiz "Sneaky Pete" Kleinow to their lineup in the late sixties. Jackson Browne's madcap sidekick David Lindley is also an ace pedal-steel player, though, as any Snob will tell you, his famous solos on *Running on Empty* are actually played on a *lap* steel, which doesn't have pedals and often conforms to a more traditional guitar shape.

Peel, David. Opportunistic Yippie nuisance and New York City street musician who briefly managed to hitch his rickety wagon to John Lennon's star. Peel began his recording career in 1968 with the novelty single "Have a Marijuana," backed by his band, the Lower East Side. Though merely a garden-variety smirky dork satirist, Peel so greatly impressed Lennon in 1971, when the ex-Beatle was new to New York and at his most susceptible to the agitprop counterculture "authenticity" of Greenwich Village longhairs, that Lennon produced Peel's album *The Pope Smokes Dope* and invited the busker-irritant to perform as a support act for the Plastic Ono Band. Though he quickly faded into deserved obscurity, Peel has recently received the RHINO Handmade treatment, with the label subversively trumpeting its rerelease of his early albums as "a must for your personal audio stash."

Peel, John. Bearded, bald, and impossibly laconic British radio personality (1939–2004) of exquisite Snob pedigree. Making his name as a DJ on pirate radio, Peel (born John Ravenscroft) was persuaded by the BBC in the late sixties to be their in-house freak, in charge of keeping the stuffy national network in touch with what the kids were into. Peel went on to embrace the first stirrings of punk, and secured his place in Snob repute when he recorded the work of many future POST-PUNK heavyweights (for example, the Jam, Siouxsie and the Banshees, and the Cure) for his radio show. Much of this music was later released on CD as the *Peel Sessions*, bringing him global renown and discreet wealth, since most of the sessions appear on a label Peel co-owned. *Yeah, the Gang of Four's first album was okay, but it couldn't touch the energy of the* Peel *sessions.*

Penn, Dan, and Spooner Oldham. Memphis-based songwriting duo invariably praised for being "real soulful for white boys." Their sixties hits include "Do Right Woman—Do Right Man," "Dark End of the Street," and "You Left the Water Running." More recently, Penn and Oldham have hit the road as performers, doing a *Storytellers*-like set of their oldies, plus some new songs. The raggedy-looking Spooner Oldham, whose funny name Rock Snobs like to utter just for the sheer frisson of it, is also an in-demand session keyboardist.

Pere Ubu. Long-running Cleveland-based avant-rock band with lovable-loser image, derived chiefly from hulking leader–front man David Thomas. Though capable of being as forbiddingly arty as contemporaries Talking Heads, Patti Smith, and TELEVISION—early albums were entitled *The Modern Dance* and *Song of the Bailing Man*, and Thomas's liner notes for the 1994 album *Raygun Suitcase* include the sentence "We live in strange times wherein Order and Meaning are terror-osterized, reduced to grist for the post-modernist vacuumizer"—Pere Ubu's pretensions are mitigated by its primal rhythms, sense of humor, and Thomas's engaging fat-guy wail.

Perry, Lee "Scratch." Mercurial, kooky, formerly forgotten reggae shaman (born in 1936) who has enjoyed new recognition since being pronounced cool by ageless Rock Snob collective the Beastie Boys in the early nineties. As a producer and as the front man for his own band, the Upsetters, Perry was, in the sixties and seventies, a prime exponent of Jamaica's swashbuckling DUB remix genre. Though his gargantuan output is as hard to penetrate as the quasi-mystical pronouncements he gives to interviewers from his home in Switzerland, he now plays to packed houses of young hipsters, few of whom actually know any of his songs.

P-Funk. Catchall term used to encompass the multifarious output of two no-longer-extant seventies funk-R&B collectives, Parliament and Funkadelic, both founded by ex-hairdresser George Clinton. Parliament began its life as a doo-wop act but progressed to elaborate concept albums about outer space, live shows featuring musicians in diapers, and a giant "mother ship" descending from an enormous denim cap. The rockier Funkadelic made LSD-tinged music that Clinton devised to be "too black for white folks and too white for black folks." Clinton, whose oeuvre has been strip-mined for samples by hip-hop artists more than any artist's besides James Brown, tours today with veterans of both bands as the P-Funk All Stars.

Phillips, John. Amiably frayed singer-songwriter, more beloved by Snobs for his dessicated post-stardom afterlife than for his early work in *Mighty Wind*–style folk groups and his mid-sixties hugeness as the Koreshian leader of the Mamas and the Papas. Descending quickly from megastardom into wanton drug abuse, Phillips, in 1970, issued a Snob-certified "lost masterpiece" called *Wolfking of L.A.* that unsparingly depicted his junked-up existence and his then-wife's miscarriage (in a song entitled "Let It Bleed, Genevieve"). Phillips also rallied to score the cult film *The Man Who Fell to Earth* and to maintain the world's coolest roster of friends, which ran the gamut from LOU ADLER to Mick Jagger (who'd coveted Phillips's daughter Mackenzie since her early teens). In 2000, Phillips finally completed the follow-up to *Wolfking* he'd begun work on in 1977, with Jagger and Keith Richards producing, but expired before its release the following year.

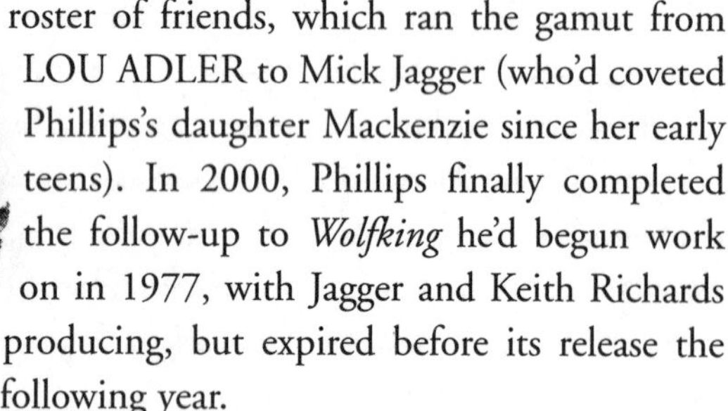
John Phillips

Philly soul. Lush R&B movement of the early to mid-seventies that, though eventually rendered obsolete by disco, anticipated that genre with its elaborate string and horn arrangements set over a driving beat. Philadelphia was home to certain influential producers—chief among them Thom Bell and the team of Kenny Gamble and Leon Huff—who sought a smoother, sweeter sound than that offered by STAX-VOLT, realizing huge hits for the O'Jays, Harold Melvin and the Blue Notes, and the Spinners. Though native Philadelphians Hall and Oates and TODD RUNDGREN were early white acolytes of Philly soul, the genre really amassed Snob cred in the early eighties, when many POST-PUNK artists chose to become crypto-soulful New Romantics rather than obtuse art-noiseniks.

Pixies, the. SEMINAL Boston-based eighties alterna-band whose formula—grunged-up pop that alternated between quiet verses and loud choruses—was transmuted into platinum sales in the nineties by the likes of Nirvana. (See also THE REPLACEMENTS.) Though the Pixies' chubby lead singer, Black Francis (né Charles Thompson IV), has enjoyed critical success under his nom-de-solo, Frank Black, and tough-gal bassist Kim Deal experienced a measure of chart success with her band the Breeders, the Pixies' four original members finally succumbed to widespread indie-world fantasizing in 2004 by embarking on a reunion tour.

Plangent. Standby rock-crit adjective used to lend a magical aura to any nonaggressive guitar-based music (even though the word's primary meaning is "loud and resounding"). *Stipe's muffled vocals and Buck's chiming,* plangent *guitar made R.E.M.'s* Murmur *one of the most auspicious debuts of the eighties.*

Post-punk. Broad term for the music that arose in the aftermath of punk rock's speedy flameout in the late seventies, as practitioned by musicians who were sympathetic to punk's aims but were too arty and clever to just gob and make noise. Much post-punk music embraced dance-funk (Talking Heads, Public Image Ltd., GANG OF FOUR), much of it reveled in absurdism and/or difficult "textures" (PERE UBU, Siouxsie and the Banshees), and most of it employed emergent synth technology, albeit not in a cheesy, mulleted way. The term has since been appropriated by historically unaware rock hacks to bestow authenticity upon such acts as Interpol and the Yeah Yeah Yeahs, who are really, in the estimate of Snobs, *post*-post-punk.

Post-rock. Amorphous genre born of rock-crit necessity in the nineties, mainly to explain to a skeptical public that the free-form, slo-mo noodlings of such semi-smart strivers as Tortoise and Low were not lazy, unstructured cop-out jams but *the music of the twenty-first century.*

Power-pop. Record-reviewer term for high-energy, Beatles-esque music made by intelligent-dork bands that, though they've given it the old college try, can't actually muster the songcraft, cleverness, vocal agility, or production ingenuity of the Beatles. First applied to early-seventies acts such as the Raspberries and BADFINGER (the latter group actually being McCartney protégés), and subsequently given a new lease on life with the nineties advent of such bands as THE WONDERMINTS and Apples in Stereo. *The Shins' debut album shimmered with pure* power-pop *exuberance.*

Power trio. Stripped-down drummer-bassist-guitarist format that experienced a mid-to-late-sixties vogue (Cream, the Jimi Hendrix Experience, BLUE CHEER, Mountain) thanks to new amplifier technology and a blues-purist re-volt against psychedelic fussiness, both of which obviated the need for a rhythm guitarist. Which was all well and good until Rush came along and managed to make even power trios sound noodly and PROG-ish.

Prince Paul. Shticky hip-hop producer, originally the DJ for the group Stetsasonic, who made his name as the production brains behind De La Soul's "Daisy Age" classic *3 Feet High and Rising*, which showcased his penchants for machismo-puncturing levity (he sampled Steely Dan and *Sesame Street* songs) and between-song comic skits, which have since become a staple/albatross of nearly every hip-hop album released. Though his output as a solo artist has been spotty, Prince Paul (last name: Huston) enjoys a certain Snob amnesty for his goofball sense of humor (his Handsome Boy Modeling School project was named after a Chris Elliott gag) and for being, along with Nelson George and Chris Rock, an unthreatening explicator of black youth culture.

Prog. Abbreviation for "progressive rock," a term used to describe the single most deplored genre of postwar pop music, inhabited by young musicians who, entranced by the eclecticism, elaborate arrangements, and ostentatious filigrees of the Beatles' *Sgt. Pepper* era, distorted their enthusiasm into a seventies morass of eternal song suites with multiple time signatures, ponderous space-cadet or medievalist lyrics, ridiculous capes and headpieces (especially where Yes' keyboard player, Rick Wakeman, was concerned), and an overall wretched bigness of sound, staging, and hair. But while prog's most egregious culprits (ELP, Yes, Jethro Tull, Rush) are easy objects of ridicule, the postmodernist penchant for rummaging through every single chapter of rock's past has made even these bands worthy of Snob investigation and adulation. *Though they're loath to admit it, Radiohead have picked up the* prog *mantle more than any other contemporary band.*

Pro Tools. Digital-audio-recording software that, since its introduction by DigiDesign in the early nineties, has become the industry standard, facilitating the production of both big-budget studio albums and home-recorded projects by dance-music specialists and disgruntled ex–group members who want to be alone. *I recorded my entire last album in my barn, using just my Mac, a Martin acoustic, and* Pro Tools.

Psych. Abbreviation for "psychedelic," most often used in hyphenated form to describe an obscure, possibly nonexistent subgenre. *"Crimson and Clover" is a bubblegum-*psych *classic; "Good Vibrations" is Wilson at his pop-*psych *zenith; our band has this sort of free-floating, bebop-*psych *sound.*

Pub rock. Frye-booted, nicotine-stained British mini-movement of the early to mid-seventies, posited by over-eager critics in rock's pre-punk dog days as the antidote to PROG and concept-album torpor. Thus were such good-natured, charisma-free chooglers as Brinsley Schwarz, Ducks Deluxe, and Bees Make Honey—who plied their trade making the rounds of saloons with Guinness-marinated carpets—dubbed the future of music. History proved otherwise, but such veterans of the pub-rock circuit as Nick Lowe (of Brinsley Schwarz), Joe Strummer (of the 101ers) and IAN DURY (of Kilburn and the High Roads) managed to shed the stigmatic stench of the ashtray and become prime movers in punk and new wave.

Ramone, Dee Dee. Junkie bassist and principal songwriter of the Ramones, né Douglas Colvin, who, more than nice Jewish boy Joey Ramone or arch-Republican Johnny Ramone, came closest to realizing the romanticized ideal of authentic punkness—much as the similarly depraved DENNIS WILSON was the only Beach Boy who really surfed. Neither his OD death just months after his 2002 induction into the Rock and Roll Hall of Fame nor his sordid past as a rent boy (as chronicled in his tart but unremittingly grisly memoirs, *Lobotomy* and *Legend of a Rock Star*, and in the Ramones song "53rd and 3rd") has deterred today's GARAGE PUNK youngsters from upholding Ramone, along with his pal Johnny Thunders of THE NEW YORK DOLLS, as the coolest people imaginable.

Dee Dee Ramone

Reich, Steve. Avant-garde composer of black raiment and academic bent, educated at Cornell and Juilliard. Reich's sixties experiments with tape loops recalled the repetitive minimalism of TERRY RILEY but added a new wrinkle, varying the tempos and start times of musical or spoken phrases to produce hypnotic, overlapping cycles that came to be known as "phase music" and went especially well with magic mushrooms; some Snobs allege that Reich is, effectively, the inventor of sampling. Possessed of a David Byrne–ish anthropological curiosity, Reich has shown a particular interest in recording African-American eccentrics, describing his 1965 recording "It's Gonna Rain" as an "auditory chalk talk" for which he "recorded a young black Pentecostal preacher who called himself Brother Walker, along with pigeons, one Sunday afternoon in Union Square." *And that was* Steve Reich *here on listener-supported WNYC . . .*

'IT'S BETTER THAN IT SOUNDS!'

Keeping the Good Snob Stuff Straight from the Crap

Though the Rock Snob prides himself on his precisely calibrated perfect musical taste, he will, occasionally, just for the sake of argument, heap fraudulent praise on music that even he knows isn't very good. His motivation? Usually, just to claim some mini-movement, usually of a revisionist bent ("Badfinger *kicked ass*!"), for himself. And, sometimes, the Snob deludes even himself, believing that, given the reputations involved, the unlistenable mulch to which he's listening simply *has* to be better than it sounds. Herewith, a consumer's guide to Snob trustworthiness.

Ten Worthwhile Snob Causes Célèbres

Syd Barrett

Nick Drake

Lee Hazlewood as producer

Fela Kuti

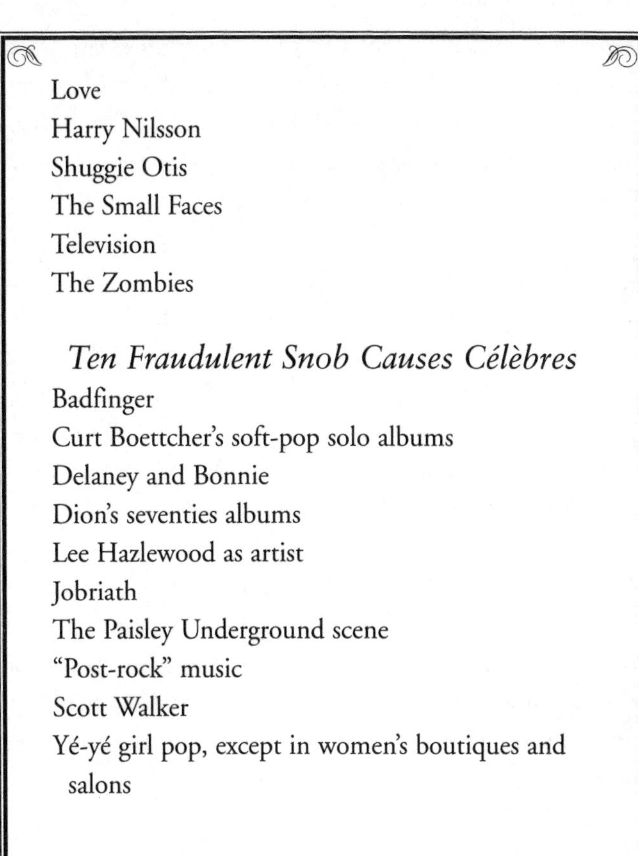

Love
Harry Nilsson
Shuggie Otis
The Small Faces
Television
The Zombies

Ten Fraudulent Snob Causes Célèbres

Badfinger
Curt Boettcher's soft-pop solo albums
Delaney and Bonnie
Dion's seventies albums
Lee Hazlewood as artist
Jobriath
The Paisley Underground scene
"Post-rock" music
Scott Walker
Yé-yé girl pop, except in women's boutiques and salons

Reid, Terry. Leather-lunged English blues shouter renowned for having turned down Jimmy Page's invitation to be the singer in the New Yardbirds, the band that became Led Zeppelin. Like SHUGGIE OTIS, a fellow former teen prodigy held in awe by the Rolling Stones (Reid opened for the Stones on the 1969 U.S. tour that ended at Altamont), Reid struggled in obscurity throughout the seventies and eighties, only to be rehabilitated, to his surprise as much as anyone else's, as a "forgotten genius." Correspondingly, his LAUREL CANYON–steeped 1976 album, *Seed of Memory*, produced by Graham Nash, has been accorded "lost masterpiece" status. Frequently confused by novice Snobs with TERRY RILEY, who is nothing like him.

Replacements, the. Shambolic eighties guitar band from Minnesota whose plaid-shirted, raspy-throated leader, Paul Westerberg, was a profound influence on both the grunge movement and the "modern rock" travesties of such bands as the Goo Goo Dolls. Westerberg broke up the band in 1990 due to poor sales and has subsequently alienated his fan base by "going soft."

Rewards repeated listens. Euphemistic phrase employed by rock critics to confer value upon a dubious musical work that, given the reputations involved, *has* to be better than it sounds. *To the unschooled novitiate,* Ice Cream for Crow *may sound like self-indulgent and studiously demented tripe, but Beefheart's swan-song LP* rewards repeated listens.

Rhino Records. Juggernaut reissue label launched out of a Los Angeles record shop in the late seventies. One of the first labels to divine the commercial appeal of kitsch, oddities, and forgotten gems, Rhino astutely assembled several compilation series of period pop, such as the *Have a Nice Day!* series of seventies hits, the *Golden Throats* series of celebrity debacles (Shatner sings "Mr. Tambourine Man"!), and more tasteful assemblages of soul and EASY LISTENING. When these approaches became old hat, Rhino branched out into high-end Snob collectibles with its Rhino Handmade imprint, which offers everything from a

$500 limited-edition multimedia bonanza of art, writings, and spoken-word recordings by Don Van Vliet, a.k.a. CAPTAIN BEEFHEART, to a $100 director's-cut DVD of the George Harrison–soundtracked Swinging London curio *Wonderwall.*

Rickenbacker. Distinctively jangly-sounding, California-manufactured electric guitar associated with mid-sixties pop in general and the "Mr. Tambourine Man"–era Byrds in particular. Retro-pop acts from Tom Petty to the Rembrandts (the *Friends* theme song) have long found the Rickenbacker—particularly in its 12-string incarnation—efficacious in evoking an era of "quality pop," much as harpsichords evoke the court of Queen Elizabeth. *The plangent chime of McGuinn's* Rickenbacker *embodied the new-dawn optimism of mid-sixties California.*

Rickenbacker

Riley, Terry. San Francisco–based hippie composer whose 1964 album, *In C,* divided listeners into champions who thought it heralded a bold new era of avant-garde Minimalism (among them Pete Townshend and the members of the SOFT MACHINE) and detractors who thought it repetitive, my-kid-could-do-that hooey. Riley went on to spearhead the New Age and raga-rock movements and has frequently collaborated with NPR megastars the Kronos Quartet. Frequently confused by novice Snobs with TERRY REID, who is nothing like him.

Riot House. Affectionate music-biz nickname for the high-rise Hyatt West Hollywood hotel on Sunset Strip, notorious in the sixties and seventies heyday of touring-Brit pomp (when it was known as the Continental Hyatt) for the debauchery that unfolded within its walls. Led Zeppelin and their entourage were renowned for shagging underage girls and riding Harleys down the halls, while Keith Richards was captured in the act of throwing a TV out of a Riot House window in *COCKSUCKER BLUES.* Per scenester-authority KIM FOWLEY, the Riot House was the site of the first-ever groupie stakeout, in 1965, when a lusty young redhead named Liz loitered outside the hotel for the express purpose of bedding a rock star, Manfred Mann's lead singer, Paul Jones.

Rock 'n' Roll Circus. Overblown 1968 *folie du cinéma* in which the Rolling Stones brought hippiedom's obsession with Victoriana to grim fruition, enlisting rock royalty (John Lennon, Eric Clapton, the Who) and a handpicked crowd of Beautiful People to participate in a muddled variety revue that failed to achieve liftoff. Filmed on a large budget under an actual big tent, *Rock 'n' Roll Circus* was intended as a TV special but never was aired, reputedly because the Stones hated their slipshod performance and were fully aware that they'd been bested by the Who, who delivered a CORUSCATING performance. Now available on video, *Rock 'n' Roll Circus* is beloved by archivalist Snobs for the opportunities it affords to see Brian Jones zoning his way out of the Stones' lineup, and for the sight of Lennon performing "Yer Blues" while backed by a rudderless supergroup dubbed the Dirty Mac.

Rocksteady. Precursor genre to reggae that allegedly came to be when, in the summer of 1966, the heat was so oppressive in the Jamaican capital of Kingston that local ska bands, seeking relief, slowed down their tempos and added languid vocals. Though Snobs reluctantly tolerated Blondie's cover of the rocksteady standard "The Tide Is High" (originally by the Paragons), they're less amused by No Doubt's purloining of the term for the title of their 2001 album.

Roland 808. Primitive yet cherished drum machine introduced by the Roland company in 1980. The user-friendly "808" combines metallic, artificial top-end sounds with a distinctive bass drum whose amniotic *whoomp* is the closest thing electronic dance music has to a trademark sound à la the RICKENBACKER's JANGLE. *The bottom end on that track is heav-ee; that's got to be an* 808 *kick in there.*

Ronson, Mick. Handsome but unassuming guitar hero of the English GLAM scene, best known for playing lead in David Bowie's Ziggy-era band, the Spiders from Mars, and for his appearance in that pansexual era's definitive tableau: the famous photograph in which Bowie-as-Ziggy, on his knees during one of Ronson's solos, appears to be fellating the guitarist. The Ronson-Bowie team went on to produce Lou Reed's finest solo hour, *Transformer*, before Bowie dissolved the Spiders, compelling Ronson to forge an alliance with another singer of luvvy theatricality, Mott the Hoople's Ian Hunter. Though in later years he functioned principally as a JOHNNY MARR–like prestige-enhancing sideman, Ronson returned to glory shortly before his 1993 death by producing longtime fan Morrissey's most edifying solo album, *Your Arsenal.*

Roots. Malleable term used to confer an air of uncorrupted integrity, regional purity, and/or a connection to music's pre-recorded era upon a musician, genre, or instrument. *Having abandoned his Buster Poindexter persona, David Johansen has rediscovered himself as a brilliant interpreter of American* roots *music.*

Rota, Nino. Italian movie composer closely associated with Federico Fellini and considered by Soundtrack Snobs to be in the league of ENNIO MORRICONE and LALO SCHIFRIN, his profile lower only because he has been dead since 1979. Most of Fellini's major works (*8½*, *La Dolce Vita*) are infused with Rota's trademark combination of fairground queasiness and nostalgic flourishes. Having also worked with Francis Ford Coppola (*The Godfather*) and Luchino Visconti (*The Leopard*), Rota is the Snob's preferred choice for evoking Cinecittà languor and decadence.

Nino Rota

Roxy Music. Flamboyant art-school GLAM-sters turned elegantly tailored crafters of atmospheric makeout pop. Snobs far prefer the out-and-out squelching weirdness of the band's first two albums, *Roxy Music* (1972) and *For Your Pleasure* (1973), during which nontrained "keyboardist" BRIAN ENO elicited odd noises from his synthesizers and pompadoured saxophonist Andy Mackay SKRONKed discordantly, to the subsequent, more accessible post-Eno albums, in which lead crooner Bryan Ferry's James Bondian cool prevailed, but both phases proved prescient and predictive of eighties trends, as did the group's penchant for using models on its covers. The non-Eno lineup reconvened in 2001 for a reunion tour, with a surprising number of Eno-era songs in the set.

Runaways, the. Feathercut all-female group of the late seventies whose jailbait image was carefully cultivated by their svengali, perennial L.A. scenester KIM FOWLEY. Intrigued by the idea of a punk girl group, Fowley assembled five Southern California teenagers, among them Joan Jett and Lita Ford, and assigned them such suggestive songs as "Cherry Bomb," which were put over with brio by the group's lingerie-clad lead singer, Cherie Currie. Though the Runaways flamed out quickly—Jett skewed punkwards, while Ford aspired to be an eighties hair-metal star—the group is viewed as a SEMINAL influence on female rock acts from the Bangles (whose bassist, Michael Steele, was deposed as the Runaways' lead singer by the more hussyish Currie) to latter-day soundalikes the Donnas.

Rundgren, Todd. Lank-haired, multifaceted big-thinker of pop-rock. Having first gained repute as the leader of the POWER-POP quartet the Nazz ("Hello, It's Me"), Rundgren established himself in the seventies as a genre-hopping, surprisingly soulful solo artist and part-time PROG-ster with his widgety side-band, Utopia. Though his 1973 opus *A Wizard, A True Star* is considered by Snobs to be among the greatest albums ever, Rundgren has compromised his ability to reach large audiences by being too egomaniacal and Buckminster Fuller–conceptual; of late, he has subjected audiences to his new "interactive" alter ego, TR-i. Nevertheless, he is much sought after as a producer, his services having been enlisted by, among others, Patti Smith, THE NEW YORK DOLLS, XTC, and JIM STEINMAN.

Sainte-Marie, Buffy. Tremulous-voiced cult vocalist of Canadian provenance and Native American stock. Sainte-Marie made her mark in the sixties with anguished, ethnocentric folk anthems such as "Now That the Buffalo's Gone" and "My Country 'Tis of Thy People You're Dying," but withdrew from recording in the mid-seventies to raise her son, to whom she assigned the name Dakota Starblanket

Wolfchild. Though her star never again rose to its early heights, Sainte-Marie made regular appearances on *Sesame Street* and maintained Snob cred by being married for a time to arranger JACK NITZSCHE, with whom she wrote the lachrymose, Oscar-winning theme for the 1982 film *An Officer and a Gentleman*.

Scelsa, Vin. Veteran New York–metro radio DJ of impeccable taste and endearingly shlubby demeanor; to Snobs, the radio equivalent of what Murray the K was to teenyboppers. Scelsa first gained widespread renown on WNEW-FM in the seventies, when, though New York was at its scuzziest and most menacing, his studio was a hospitable, homey place where anyone from John Lennon to Joey Ramone might drop in to shoot the breeze and play their favorite SIDES. Scelsa has since formalized this format as the host of the Saturday-night program *Idiot's Delight*, now on public radio, in which coolpersons from all walks of the arts (Kurt Vonnegut, Steve Buscemi, MARIANNE FAITHFULL, Peter Buck, Gus Van Sant, etc.) schmooze agreeably with Vin and bask in his Jersey-guy unpretentiousness.

Schifrin, Lalo. Modish Argentinean film scorer, second only to ENNIO MORRICONE on the modern-cool index. Known for his urgent, suspense-stoking compositions of the sixties and seventies (for *Bullitt, Dirty Harry, Enter the Dragon*, and the TV show *Mannix*, among other commissions), Schifrin found his status among postmodernist Snobs further enhanced when MTV-spawned director Brett Ratner asked him to score 1998's surprise hit *Rush Hour*. Schifrin's oeuvre recently received the

Lalo Schifrin

lavish-repackage treatment from Warner Bros. *That orchestral break on McCartney's "Live and Let Die" has* Schifrin *written all over it.*

Section, the. Nickname for an agglomeration of slick Los Angeles sessioneers—guitarist Danny Kortchmar, bassist Leland Sklar, drummer Russ Kunkel, and keyboardist Craig Doerge—whose ubiquity on seventies singer-songwriter albums (by James Taylor, Carole King, Jackson Browne, and Warren Zevon, among others) and denimy, hirsute appearances marked them as the embodiment of that era's mellowness–versus–cocaine paranoia dialectic.

Seminal. Catchall adjective employed by rock writers to describe any group or artist in on a trend too early to sell any records. *The Germs were a* seminal *L.A. punk band, but guitarist Pat Smear didn't realize any riches until he joined Nirvana.*

Shaw, Greg. Astute Los Angeles scenester (1949–2004) who allegedly coined the term POWER-POP in his rock fanzine *Who Put the Bomp*, which flourished in the seventies as a sort of West Coast answer to *CRAWDADDY!* (The 'zine's esoteric name came from a BRILL BUILDING–era novelty song by Barry Mann and Gerry Goffin.) In 1974, Shaw started up the independent Bomp! label, which, though it enjoyed its greatest influence in the late-seventies heyday of such SEMINAL L.A. punk acts as the Germs, the Dead Boys, and Stiv Bators, persisted into the twenty-first century under the direction of its founder, who, well into middle age, still sports the regulation Byrdsian pageboy 'do required of power-popsters.

THE ROCK SNOB FILMOGRAPHY

The Films That Every Snob Must Claim to Have Seen

Apocalypse Now (1979). Even the Doors-averse admire Coppola's masterly deployment of "The End."

Christiane F. (1981). Unwatchable German film about a teen smack addict—but cool Bowie concert sequence!

Cocksucker Blues (1972). Seldom-screened, not-available-on-video Rolling Stones debauch-umentary.

The Decline of Western Civilization (1981). Penelope Spheeris documentary about L.A. punk scene, followed by an infinitely more watchable sequel about the subsequent hair-metal scene.

Don't Look Back (1967). D. A. Pennebaker documentary of Zimmy's 1965 visit to Swinging London. Contains the song with that "title card" sequence.

Eat the Document (1972). Opaque, seldom-screened Pennebaker documentary of Zimmy's 1966 visit to

Swinging London. Features John Lennon, acid, vomit.

Expresso Bongo (1959). English artifact of pre-Beatles Swinging Soho scene, with Cliff Richard.

Head (1968). The Monkees' career-ending freakout.

How I Won the War (1967). Richard Lester film that occasioned John Lennon's transformation into his skinny, bespectacled late-sixties self.

Je T'Aime Moi Non Plus (1976). Serge Gainsbourg vanity pic with lots of nudity.

Journey Through the Past (1972). The first of Neil Young's sludgy home movies under the pseudonym Bernard Shakey, in this case focusing on the CSNY years. Better than *Rust Never Sleeps* and *Greendale*.

The Man Who Fell to Earth (1976). Autistically edited culmination of Bowie's space-alien obsession, courtesy of art-house unusualist Nic Roeg.

Masked and Anonymous (2003). Bonkers Zimmy crypto-autobiography with all-star cast and Bob sporting his latter-day cowboy wardrobe.

O Brother, Where Art Thou? (2000). The Coen Brothers film that wrested Americana from the grip of Snobs and took it mainstream.

Performance (1970). Nic Roeg movie with Mick Jagger, threesomes, drugs, and Cockney ruffians.

Pink Floyd—The Wall (1982). Dystopian downer film with Bob Geldof. A staple of midnight cinema.

Renaldo and Clara (1978). Impenetrable four-hours-plus Zimmy opus.

Repo Man (1984). Anomic L.A. New Wave farce overseen by recovering Monkee Michael Nesmith and featuring the posthumously acclaimed L.A. punk strivers the Circle Jerks.

Riot on Sunset Strip (1967). Crappy but beloved Stripsploitation film with title song by the proto-punk losers the Standells.

Skidoo (1968). Bizarre kitsch meta-gangster pic with music by Harry Nilsson (who sings the credits aloud) and the unedifying sight of Jackie Gleason and Groucho Marx going psychedelic. Directed by Otto Preminger, no less.

Superstar: The Karen Carpenter Story (1987). Forty-minute short by Todd Haynes, enacted entirely by Barbie dolls; Richard Carpenter's threat of legal action instantly ended the film's theatrical release and made it a coveted Snob bootleg.

The T.A.M.I. Show (1964). Heady summit of Motown, British Invasion, and U.S. surf-pop talents that is all the more intriguing for its commercial unavailability.

This Is Spinal Tap (1984). Still the funniest Rock Snob film ever. Period metalheads thought it was real.

200 Motels (1971). Frank Zappa–directed nonsense film with Ringo appearance.

Two-Lane Blacktop (1971). Drag-racing period piece starring James Taylor and Dennis Wilson, outshone by *Easy Rider* but much, much cooler to Snobs.

Side. Grating term for a single, usually used in a tone of especially contemptible knowingness. *Though ignored at the time of its release, "The Porpoise Song" was one of the Monkees' greatest* sides.

Silverhead. Early-seventies English GLAM-rock band of no discernible talent except for proving that any skinny young Englishman milling around Los Angeles in that era could shag as many tasty American birds as he desired; as such, an antecedent of the nineties quasi-GLAM band Spacehog, a combo from Leeds that, despite minimal commercial impact, infiltrated the New York–L.A. fashionista set and ensorcelled Liv Tyler into marrying one of its members. Silverhead lead vocalist Michael Des Barres landed the ultimate L.A. groupie trophy, the infamous Miss Pamela—who as Pamela Des Barres would write the famous memoir *I'm With the Band*—and later achieved an acutely mid-eighties kind of success as an actor on *Miami Vice* and as Robert Palmer's substitute in the touring version of the Power Station.

Simone, Nina. Temperamental singer-pianist of shiver-inducing intensity, known, by her record company's proclamation, as the "High Priestess of Soul." Born Eunice Waymon in North Carolina, Simone emerged in the late fifties as a cabaret-style "interpreter" but matured in the sixties into a pissed-off civil-rights advocate and stylistic polymath, recording "Don't Let Me Be Misunderstood" and "The House of the Rising Sun" before the Animals did, and her own "Mississippi Goddam" after the murder of Medgar Evers. Disgusted with American racism, Simone renounced the USA in 1969 and ultimately settled in France, where, until her death in 2003, she was worshipped from afar by Snobs who regard her as the only contemporary recording artist truly worthy of the word *diva.*

'68 Comeback Special. Nickname for a television special that originally carried the simple title *Elvis.* Upheld by Snobs as Elvis Presley's last great flourish of brilliance before getting fat and inordinately chummy with Richard Nixon, the special, which aired on NBC in December 1968, saw Presley temporarily liberating himself from the odious grind of B-movies and reclaiming his relevance and sensuality in the Beatle era—growing out his sideburns again, wearing tight leathers, and, of the most musicological importance, reuniting with his fifties bandmates Scotty Moore and D. J. Fontana for a proto-*Unplugged,* ROOTSy revisitation of old rockabilly numbers. Though *Elvis* had no shortage of the sort of overwrought, unintentionally funny production numbers endemic to TV at that time, the stripped-down segment, only a fragment of which was seen in the original special, has since become a phenomenon of its own as a full-length video entitled *Elvis—One Night with You.*

Skronk. Nonsense crit term used to describe the sort of atonal emanation heard routinely in instrumental "performance pieces" at THE KNITTING FACTORY. Among the early popularizers of the word was *The New York Times*'s Robert Palmer, who in 1985 used *skronk* to describe a dissonant guitar sound. *Braxton's sax solo grew more dazzling and cathartic with every fillip, blast, and* skronk.

Sly and Robbie. Joint handle of drummer Lowell "Sly" Dunbar and bassist Robert Shakespeare; also known as the Riddim Twins. Gaining repute as Peter Tosh's rhythm section in the late seventies, Sly and Robbie were coveted in the early eighties by superstars looking to infuse their sessions with reggae flava, among them Mick Jagger, Bob Dylan, and SERGE GAINSBOURG. *Grace Jones's "Pull Up to the Bumper" positively throbs with the rock-hard riddims of* Sly and Robbie.

Small Faces, the. Dapper, diminutive sixties quartet that brought some authentic East End swagger to the suspiciously posh Swinging London scene. Long relegated to rock's second or third rank, the Small Faces, buoyed by the Britpop craze of the mid-nineties, have been rehabilitated into "the most underrated band of the late sixties" (as per *MOJO* magazine). Emerging mid-decade as mod standard-bearers with such exuberantly horny teen anthems as "Sha-La-La-La-Lee" and "What'cha Gonna Do About It," the band cemented its Snob status in 1968 by forsaking amphetamines for acid and recording their PSYCH-pop classic, *Ogden's Nut Gone Flake*, mint copies of which, in the original circular sleeve (designed to resemble a tobacco tin), are as cherished as the elusive "butcher sleeve" copies of the Beatles' *Yesterday and Today*. By decade's end, the group's napalm-throated singer, Steve Marriot, was enjoying U.S. stardom with Peter Frampton in Humble Pie, while bandmates Ian McLagan, Kenney Jones, and Ronnie Lane joined fellow mod refugees Ronnie Wood and Rod Stewart to form the Faces, a booze-rock combo of short life span but lasting Snob repute.

Soft Boys, the. SEMINAL English pop group of the late seventies that was the launchpad of both the beloved indie eccentric Robyn Hitchcock and the bangs-wearing guitarist Kimberley Rew, who went on to cofound mid-eighties retro-popsters Katrina and the Waves. Though the

Soft Boys' sound was a genial amalgam of SYD BARRETT–era Pink Floyd, Byrdsian RICKENBACKER JANGLE, Lennonesque wit, and CAPTAIN BEEFHEART–like abandon, it was suicidally ill-matched to the Year Zero ethos of the POST-PUNK era. Frequently confused by novice Snobs with the SOFT MACHINE.

Soft Machine, the. SEMINAL English psychedelic group of the late sixties that was the launchpad of both the beloved indie eccentric ROBERT WYATT and the foppish pop sybarite Kevin Ayers. In addition, the Soft Machine's sometime sax player, Elton Dean, was the person from whom a bespectacled aspiring pop star named Reginald Dwight pinched half of his stage name. Though their heyday ended around 1971, the band persisted for another ten years in various lineups as a noodly jazz-fusion and PROG band. Frequently confused by novice Snobs with the SOFT BOYS.

Sonic Youth. Agelessly hip guitar-noise combo that rose in 1981 from the ashes of the NO WAVE movement. Founded by GLENN BRANCA disciples Thurston Moore and Lee Ranaldo, along with Moore's indie-pinup wife, Kim Gordon, the group (soon to be joined by boyish drummer Steve Shelley) achieved critical mass with 1988's *Daydream Nation*, upheld by Snobs as the decade's greatest double album and a landmark of Downtown NYC gallery-rock. Relentlessly curatorial in nature, the group's members are compulsive anointers, collectors, and tastemakers, each with various side-gigs: Moore as the overseer of the agitprop Protest Records; Gordon as an artist and sometime fashion designer; Ranaldo as a freelance noisenik, writer, and conceptual artist; and Shelley as the overseer of the boutique label Smells Like Records. In 2001, the band even collected a fifth member, maestro of difficult-but-rewarding music JIM O'ROURKE.

South by Southwest. Annual Austin, Texas, music festival–cum–industry convention that, since its inception in 1987, has become the prime one-stop showcase for ascendant indie talent; a sort of Rock Snob analogue to the Sundance Film Festival (though South by Southwest has expanded its mandate to include film and new media). Each year, over a thousand acts perform on more than fifty stages. Like all things that began in indie-upstart fashion, such as Sub Pop records, Lollapalooza, and rock itself, South by Southwest (known in shorthand as SXSW) is lamented by Snobs for having been "corporatized" and for not being the loose, scrappy free-for-all it once was, though it's still wont to offer soon-to-be-big bands their first national exposure, as such alums as the Yeah Yeah Yeahs, Norah Jones, and the Strokes can attest.

Southern-fried boogie. Ancient rock-hack phrase, originally used to describe the music of hirsute white electric-blues bands of early-seventies vintage, such as ZZ Top, the Outlaws, and the Allman Brothers, but dusted off recently to describe the new music of hirsute white youngsters of early-seventies ethos, such as Kid Rock and Kings of Leon. *Fresh from the backwoods of Tennessee, Kings of Leon blew away the crowd with their hickory-smoked brand of* southern-fried boogie.

Sparks. Camp-oddity duo of baffling durability, consisting of brothers Ron Mael (keyboards) and Russell Mael (vocals). Though the Maels are from Los Angeles, their most loyal constituency is in Britain, where, at the height of the GLAM era, they scored a No. 2 hit with the over-the-top mock-operatic single "This Town Ain't Big Enough for the Both of Us" and mesmerized *Top of the Pops* viewers with their bizarre appearance: Ron, with his Hitler/Chaplin mustache, slicked-back hair, and poker-faced demeanor, and Russell, with his Shirley Temple ringlets and yelping, hyperactive singing. At the height of their success, in 1974, the Maels tried to poach Queen's guitarist, Brian May, on the grounds that May's group was "washed up." Sparks perseveres to this day, thanks to a corps of starry-eyed devotees that includes Morrissey.

Sparks

Spence, Skip. Canadian-born musician and acid casualty who, like ROKY ERICKSON, is often held up as a North American answer to SYD BARRETT. Spence played drums for Jefferson Airplane before achieving greater fame as a guitarist for the psychedelic band Moby Grape. After quitting the Grape and sojourning for a time at New York's Bellevue Hospital, Spence retired to Nashville, where, wearing pajamas, he recorded a bunch of dithering, fried-brain song fragments, out of which was constructed the 1969 album *Oar*. Though it sank without a trace upon its release, *Oar* was subsequently rereleased in 1991, and today is held up by overeager Rock Snobs as a lost classic. Spence, to his credit, professed before his death in 1999 that he was, in a friend's words, "mildly puzzled by all the hoopla surrounding *Oar*."

Stanley Brothers, the. Bluegrass duo formed in 1946 by Virginian brothers Carter (guitar, lead vocals) and Ralph (banjo, harmony vocals). With their backing group, the Clinch Mountain Boys, the Stanleys were a fixture on the college and folk-festival circuit until Carter's death in 1966. Thereafter, Ralph persevered as an elder statesman of mountain music, his fan base limited to the country cognoscenti until he attracted national attention with his warbly, shamanistic a cappella rendition of "O Death" on the *O Brother, Where Art Thou?* soundtrack. Though known now even to Starbucks baristas and entertainment lawyers, Ralph is still cherished by Heritage Snobs who like to enthuse about how his banjo technique "ingeniously fuses the old-time clawhammer approach with the three-finger style of Earl Scruggs."

Stax/Volt. Composite term for two Memphis-based soul labels of the sixties, Stax Records and its subsidiary, Volt, whose releases, by the likes of Sam & Dave, Otis Redding, and Rufus Thomas, provided a rawer, grittier counterpart to the more polished black pop of Motown. Rock Snobs are particularly enamored of Stax/Volt's crack house band, Booker T. and the MGs, and its equally adept horn section, the Mar-Keys. *When I saw all those great* Stax/Volt *players backing up Belushi and Aykroyd, I didn't know whether to laugh or cry.*

Steinman, Jim. White-maned impresario of epic schlock-rock, most notably Meat Loaf's *Bat Out of Hell* albums. Obsessed, like Phil Spector, with the cathedralesque sonic ambition of Richard Wagner's music, Steinman used his training in musical theater (he was a protégé of Joseph Papp's) and Meat Loaf's foghorn voice to fashion enormous-sounding (and enormously titled) pop operettas such as "Paradise by the Dashboard Light" and "You Took the

Words Right Out of My Mouth" in the late seventies, and repeated the trick in the early nineties with "I'd Do Anything for Love (But I Won't Do That)" and "Objects in the Rear View Mirror May Appear Closer than They Are." Far from being appalled, the Snob cognoscenti gushed their admiration: TODD RUNDGREN produced Steinman's sole solo album, while Courtney Love has praised him as "a genius."

Stockhausen, Karlheinz. Avant-garde German composer and early electronic-music enthusiast whose sound collages and forays into *musique concrète* have impressed pop disciples ranging from the Beatles (whose "Revolution 9" was a very Stockhausian piece of art gibberish) to JIM O'ROURKE. Already given to making extraordinarily pretentious, *Sprockets*-like pronouncements—being an avant-garde German composer and all—Stockhausen forfeited all civilian goodwill when he publicly declared the 9/11 terrorist attacks to be "the greatest work of art imaginable for the whole cosmos."

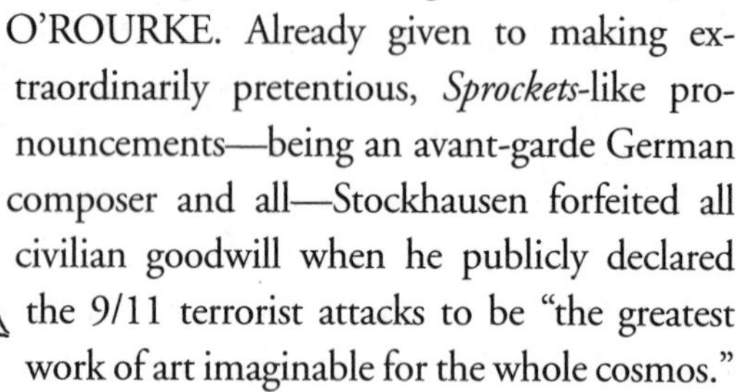

Karlheinz Stockhausen

Stone Canyon Band. Country-rock vehicle for Rick "Formerly Known as Ricky" Nelson, who sought to overcome his teen-idol image from the *Ozzie and Harriet* days by repackaging himself in the LAUREL CANYON singer-songwriter mold. For a brief moment, Nelson succeeded, with the Stone Canyon Band's "Garden Party," a bitter swipe at rock-nostalgia shows, reaching the Top 10 in 1972. But Nelson never again matched this achievement, fading out just as his Hollywood-country compatriots, the Eagles (featuring his former bass player, Randy Meisner), ascended to Lear jet–and–Lafite supremacy.

Stooges, the. Filthy-sounding, drug-addled late-sixties–early-seventies Detroit band fronted by charismatic, self-mutilating singer Iggy Pop, né James Osterberg. The Stooges' primal, three-chord rock and Pop's naughty, nihilistic lyrics (on such songs as "I Wanna Be Your Dog" and "Your Pretty Face Is Going to Hell") helped form the template for punk. *Degenerate drummer seeks like-minded fuck ups to jam and kick ass like the* Stooges.

Sugar Hill Records. New Jersey label responsible for releasing the first hip-hop record, "Rapper's Delight," a CHIC-sampling 1979 hit by the makeshift Sugarhill Gang. Run by Sylvia Robinson, a seasoned songwriter and performer (from 1957's "Love Is Strange" to 1973's "Pillow Talk") and her Mob-acquainted husband, Joe, Sugar Hill enjoyed near-monopoly status during hip-hop's oldest-of-OLD-SCHOOL phase, signing acts such as Grandmaster Flash and the Furious Five, Funky Four Plus One, and Spoonie Gee to allegedly onerous contracts. But by 1983, the Robinsons had licensed their struggling label to MCA Records, and later claimed that the corporation was systematically ripping them off.

Suicide. Attitudinous Noo Yawk electro-punk duo of the seventies, composed of runty sculptor Alan Vega and his synth-playing sidekick, Martin Rev. Resembling a consumptive, leathered-up Chico Marx, Vega was so confrontational in performance that he was anathema even to other punks (who were also wary of the group's tinny, guitar-free sound), but he is today considered the affable grandpappy of a variety of movements, from techno to ELECTROCLASH. Still huge in France, Suicide issued its inevitable reunion album, *American Supreme*, in 2002.

THE SNOB CHEAT SHEET FOR CONFUSING SIMILARITIES

Nick Cave is a tall, gaunt Australian gloom-rocker who has written such songs as "The Mercy Seat." **Nick Kent** is a wizened, gaunt English rock writer who was central to the seventies "golden age" of *New Musical Express*. **Nik Cohn** is another English rock writer whose most famous works are the book *Awopbopaloobop Alopbamboom* and the *New York* magazine article that was the basis for *Saturday Night Fever*. **Nick Drake** was a willowy, dulcet English folkie who died in the early seventies and whose work is discovered each year by college freshpersons of delicate constitution.

Bill Frisell is the guitar virtuoso who first made his name in the early eighties as part of New York's avant-jazz scene. **Bill Laswell** is the bass virtuoso whose early-eighties collaborations with Herbie Hancock (on "Rockit"), David Byrne, and Brian Eno cemented his status as the elder statesman of avant-dance.

Bill Bruford is the prog drummer known for his work with King Crimson and Yes. **Bill Buford** is the writer who used to be an editor at *Granta* and *The New Yorker*, and who wrote a book about soccer hooliganism called *Among the Thugs.*

John Hiatt is the affably rootsy, gracefully aging American singer-songwriter whose song "Thing Called Love" was winningly covered by Bonnie Raitt. **John Prine** is the affably rootsy, gracefully aging American singer-songwriter whose song "Angel from Montgomery" was winningly covered by Bonnie Raitt. **John Martyn** is the affably rootsy, gracefully aging Scottish singer-songwriter whose catalogue is ripe for the Bonnie Raitt treatment.

The Soft Boys were a melodic British pop group whose heyday was in the late seventies. They re-formed in the early twenty-first century, and their most famous member is Robyn Hitchcock. **The Soft Machine** was a noodly, well-schooled British psychedelic group whose heyday was in the late sixties. They persisted in various lineups until the early eighties, and their most famous alumnus is Robert Wyatt.

Townes Van Zandt was the Texas singer-songwriter who wrote "Pancho and Lefty." **Steven Van Zandt** is the E Street Band guitarist and *Sopranos* actor who also goes by the name Little Steven. **Ronnie Van Zant** was the menacing lead singer of Lynyrd Skynyrd who died in a 1977 plane crash. **Van Dyke Parks** is the baroque-pop wordsmith who collaborated with Brian Wilson on *Smile.*

Johnny Winter is the hirsute albino blues guitarist who was a huge touring attraction in the seventies and who produced Muddy Waters's *Hard Again* comeback album in 1977. **Edgar Winter** is the still more hirsute albino saxophonist whose Edgar Winter Group scored a 1973 hit with the deathless car-radio anthem "Free Ride." Edgar is Johnny's younger brother. **Johnny Rivers** is a sixties Sunset Strip guitar-slinger who sneaked a bunch of lackluster cover versions into the Top 40, as well as the timeless "Secret Agent Man."

Sundazed. Geek-run reissue label, based in upstate New York, that threatens to overtake RHINO RECORDS in the memory-recycling stakes, offering, in the words of its own Web site, "the most fuzz-damaged garage bands, reverb-drenched surf combos, far-out swamis of mind expansion . . . and chart-topping pop heroes in the known universe." In addition to reissuing on CD the deeply misunderstood albums of such essential Snob artists as CURT BOETTCHER, GRAM PARSONS, and SKIP SPENCE, Sundazed also offers a line of limited-edition "180-gram vinyl" versions of such masterworks as WILCO's *Yankee Hotel Foxtrot* and the Young Rascals' debut LP.

Sun-drenched harmonies. Default rock-crit phrase, in renewed vogue as more and more rock acts attempt to emulate the vocal-arrangement acuity of BRIAN WILSON and such LAUREL CANYON stalwarts as the Eagles and Crosby, Stills and Nash. *Sheryl Crow's* C'mon C'mon *is a summery delight, its infectious tunes overlaid with* sun-drenched harmonies.

Sun Ra. Chicago-based jazz pianist and arranger (real name: Herman "Sonny" Blount) who started out in the fifties as a Thelonious Monk acolyte but reinvented himself in the sixties as a quasi-psychedelic space-cadet bandleader. Wearing homeless-nut threads evocative of both CAPTAIN BEEFHEART's and P-FUNK's absurd finery, Sun Ra presided over an "Intergalactic Arkestra" that played noisy free jazz for two or three generations of swaying white druggie congregants at summer festivals. He died in 1993.

Sylvester. Aggressively queeny black disco singer of the late seventies (1947–1988), posthumously regarded by dance-music Snobs and queer theorists as the spangly materfamilias of modern hedonistic club culture. (He paraded about in drag years before RuPaul and OutKast's Andre 3000.) Though such amyl-popper anthems as "You Make Me Feel (Mighty Real)" and "Dance (Disco Heat)" were never huge chart hits, they won the crucial appreciation of the Studio 54 cognoscenti, making Sylvester a chic name-

Sylvester

drop in Manhattan to this day. His hefty backing singers, Martha Wash and Izora Rhodes, later scored their own gay-disco hit as the Weather Girls, with "It's Raining Men."

Talk Talk. British New Romantic band that seemed insignificant in its early-eighties heyday, but posthumously emerged as a Snob favorite on account of its brooding, commercially disastrous 1988 opus, *Spirit of Eden*. Cynically conceived in 1982 as Human League–Duran Duran synth-pop bandwagoneers, Talk Talk wandered off the beaten path as the decade advanced, embracing Snob instrumentation (double bass, HAMMOND B3 organ), sullen lyrics, and an embargo on band photos. Public indifference sealed Talk Talk's status as prescient musical martyrs, particularly in light of No Doubt's smash cover of their song "It's My Life" and Radiohead's latter-day success with similar "textures" and "strategies."

T.A.M.I. Show, the. SEMINAL concert movie, originally filmed for television in Santa Monica in 1964, that features a mind-boggling cross-section of surf-pop acts (Jan and Dean, the Beach Boys), soul and Motown acts (the Supremes, James Brown, Marvin Gaye, the Miracles), and British Invasion bands (the Rolling Stones, Billy J. Kramer and the Dakotas, Gerry and the Pacemakers). Like *COCKSUCKER BLUES*, *The T.A.M.I. Show* remains unavailable on video and is only screenable at film societies, enhancing its Snob allure. The show was directed by Steve Binder, later to helm Elvis Presley's '68 COMEBACK SPECIAL, and the theme music was composed by JACK NITZSCHE.

Technics SL-1200 Mark 2. Unassuming turntable that began its life as a hi-fi component for 1972 Hef aspirants, but, thanks to the sturdiness of its belt drive, was later adopted by whiplash-wristed club DJs, who linked pairs of them to a mixer. To this day, the SL-1200 is the prime instrument of turntablists worldwide. Though hip-hop and dance music tend to be weak spots for the Rock Snob, knowing about the SL-1200 Mark 2 is still de rigueur, a touchstone of dance-culture insiderism. *Dude! I just got an* SL-1200 *for the apartment!*

Television. Late-seventies guitar band lumped into the New York punk movement by dint of connections to the CBGB's scene (Blondie, Talking Heads, Ramones) but actually wont to do unpunk things such as play eight-minute songs featuring noodly guitar duels between second banana Richard Lloyd and ornery, beanpole-ish front man Tom Verlaine (whose ex-girlfriend Patti Smith described his playing as sounding "like a thousand bluebirds screaming"). Considered by Rock Snobs to be more important than any other New York band of the era, despite having released just two albums, 1977's *Marquee Moon* and 1978's *Adventure* (plus an obligatory 1990s reunion album).

Thompson, Richard. Wry, bearded singer-songwriter-guitarist and veteran of SEMINAL British folk group the Fairport Convention; unaccountably deified by rock critics for his intelligent yet never transcendentally great albums. (*Rolling Stone* named *Shoot Out the Lights*, the 1982 album he made with his soon-to-be ex-wife, Linda, as that year's best.) As such, Thompson has provided the template for a slew of younger, similarly overpraised

Richard Thompson

troubadours such as Freedy Johnston, Vic Chesnutt, and Ron Sexsmith.

Tighten Up. SEMINAL series of cheapo reggae compilations issued in England by Trojan Records in the late sixties and early seventies, each volume offering a sampling of Jamaican singles and a comely lady on the cover. Though historically important as the blueprint for the interracial ska-pop boom of the late seventies (the Specials, Madness, the Beat), the *Tighten Up* series is today valued more as a name-drop for pigmentation-challenged Snobs bluffing their way toward hipster credibility. *Man, there's nothing better than cooling out in my yard with a couple of Red Stripes and a boom box playing* Tighten Up Volume 3.

Tinnitus. "Ringing ear" syndrome common among rock musicians and aging Snobs; an occupational hazard of playing heavily amplified music or listening to loud playback on headphones. (Some BLUE CHEER fans actually boast of the "tinnitus buzz" the band's notoriously loud concerts have left them with.) Tinnitus's most famous sufferer is the Who's Pete Townshend, who no longer wears an in-ear monitor in concert and experiences horrific postshow pain. Ex-president/saxophonist Bill Clinton is also said to be a sufferer.

ToeRag Studios. Tatty, reverse-chic London recording facility that uses only vintage equipment, such as NEUMANN microphones, VOX AC-30 amplifiers, and LESLIE speakers. Founded in 1992, ToeRag became a Snob byword with the release of White Stripes' *Elephant* album, which was recorded there, and whose song "Ball and Biscuit" takes its name from an old-fashioned microphone

T

(more clinically known as an STC 4021) suspended from ToeRag's ceiling.

T.O.N.T.O.'s Expanding Headband. Weird-beard duo composed of two assistants to synthesizer pioneer Dr. Robert MOOG, Malcolm Cecil and Robert Margouleff, who met in the late sixties while working on a new synthesizer—to be called the Original New Timbral Orchestra—that Moog himself thought substandard and disowned. Unbowed, Cecil and Margouleff persevered with the contraption, recording blurping, heaving music under the T.O.N.T.O. banner and attracting the attention of Stevie Wonder, who roped the pair in to assist on his transitional 1971 album *Music of My Mind* and subsequent future-funk classics. The original T.O.N.T.O. hardware is said to reside with ex-Devo singer and current soundtrack titan Mark Mothersbaugh.

Trad jazz. Shorthand for *traditional jazz*, denoting the melodic, un-SKRONKy music of such pioneers as Jelly Roll Morton, Louis Armstrong, and Duke Ellington, as well as that of such pre-bebop stars as Lester Young and Coleman Hawkins. Often cited as an influence by sentimental baby boomer rockers. *I spent me childhood raiding me dad's* trad jazz *records and trying to mimic Sidney Bechet's clarinet with me mouth organ.*

T. Rex. Undisputed prime movers of GLAM, presided over by Marc Bolan (né Feld), a tiny, corkscrew-curled Jewish kid from South London who, at the dawn of the seventies, forsook the acoustic, Tolkienish PSYCH-whimsy of his then band, Tyrannosaurus Rex, and reinvented himself as a boa-wearing, top-hatted preen-rocker—a makeover, literally and artistically, whose significance was not lost on Bolan's still long-tressed friend David Bowie. The reconstituted, abbreviated T. Rex scored almost instant success with its nonsensical but insistently catchy single "Bang a Gong (Get It On)" and its parent album, *Electric Warrior* (1971), establishing Bolan, briefly, as Britain's biggest rock star. But Bolan quickly succumbed to serious alcoholism, Keith Moon–ish tomfoolery, and artistic decline before dying in a car crash in 1977.

Troggs, the. Atavistic Brit yokels who hit transatlantic pay dirt in 1966 with "Wild Thing," a prehensile stomper whose classic status was confirmed by a Jimi Hendrix cover. Led by the splendidly monikered Reg Presley, the Troggs went on to record several hits of surprising delicacy, one of which, "Love Is All Around," was later covered by R.E.M. Reg and his coarse mates live on in Snob legend through a widely circulated bootleg known as "The Troggs Tape," twelve minutes of sixties-vintage, potty-mouthed squabbling that foreshadowed both *This Is Spinal Tap* and Oasis's Gallagher brothers.

Tropicalia. Term describing both a 1968 compilation of avant-pop released in Brazil and the subsequent movement it inspired. Mixing Brazilian rhythms with Anglo-American songcraft and hippie flourishes, Tropicalia—and its foremost practitioners, such as the Rock Snob cult fave Tom Ze—gained new currency in the late nineties thanks to youthful champions such as Beck, who included a song called "Tropicalia" on his album *Mutations*.

Troutman, Roger. Flamboyant synth-funk producer and leader of early-eighties funk band Zapp, best known for its quasi-underground hits “More Bounce to the Ounce” and “Dance Floor.” Troutman’s trademark kitsch-futuristic sound was enhanced by his processing of his vocals through a VOCODER, which he referred to as a “Ghetto Robot.” Though his career was resuscitated by his appearance on Dr. Dre and Tupac’s 1996 hit, “California Love,” Troutman died tragically three years later when he was gunned down by his brother-manager, who then committed suicide.

Turner, Ike. Misogynistic R&B bandleader who, despite his amply documented long-term abuse of vocalist wife Tina, retains respect in Snob circles for having been the driving force behind “Rocket 88,” the 1951 Kings of Rhythm SIDE widely regarded as the first rock-and-roll recording. Though Turner endured the *A Star Is Born*–style humiliation of sitting in jail (on a drug conviction) in 1991 while his glamorous, multiplatinum-selling ex-wife celebrated their acceptance into the Rock and Roll Hall of Fame, a forgiving music industry bestowed a Grammy nomination upon him in 2001, and he continues to be a live draw, especially among youngsters who regard him as a found-object curiosity.

Van Zandt, Townes. Lanky Texan singer-songwriter in the country-folk idiom who, like GRAM PARSONS, exuded a hard-drinkin’, ramblin’-man aura despite coming from a wealthy family. Best known for his song “Pancho and Lefty,” a huge country hit for Willie Nelson and Merle Haggard in 1981, Van Zandt the performer never rose above cult-artist status, and died a HARRY NILSSON–like alcohol-related death in the 1990s. Frequently confused by novice Snobs with eccentric L.A. scenester

Townes Van Zandt

VAN DYKE PARKS, immolated Lynyrd Skynyrd singer Ronnie Van Zant, and Springsteen sideman/*Sopranos* actor Steven Van Zandt, none of whom is anything like him.

Varèse, Edgard. Contentious French avant-garde composer (1883–1965) of dissonant, polyrhythmic "symphonies," dismissed in his early adulthood as a nutball for arguing that the future of music lay in electronic machines, but embraced late in his life and posthumously by heavy musos as a maverick and electro-visionary. Frank Zappa used one of Varèse's characteristically febrile quotes, "The present-day composer refuses to die!" as an epigraph on the sleeves of all his early albums, and spent the last months of his life recording Varèse's works as he imagined Varèse wanted them to sound, with technologies not available during the composer's lifetime. It's also said that you can hear a muffled voice saying "Can you dig it, Varèse?" on Pink Floyd's 1969 album *Ummagumma*.

Vocoder. Timeless cyberpop gadget that distorts the human voice into a cold, robotic bleat; used archly on Laurie Anderson's "O Superman" and throughout KRAFTWERK's oeuvre, funkily in the work of Zapp's ROGER TROUTMAN, and kitschily in Madonna's "Music," Cher's "Believe," and the Beastie Boys' "Intergalactic." Developed at Bell Laboratories in the thirties as a telecommunications aid, the vocoder's potential as a musical device was first recognized, appropriately enough, by a German phonetics professor who attended a demonstration by the device's inventor, Homer Dudley, at Bonn University. *I thought Neil Young had lost it when he did all the singing on his* Trans *album through a* vocoder.

Voormann, Klaus. Teutonic rock demi-legend regarded by Snobs as being somewhere between the seventh and ninth Beatle. As an art student in early-sixties Hamburg, Voormann befriended the nascent, leather-clad Fab Four and introduced them to his then girlfriend, Astrid Kirchherr, later to invent the "Beatle cut." Voormann went on to design the cover of the group's 1966 album, *Revolver*, and to play bass guitar on post-Beatle albums by Harrison, Starr, and Lennon, most memorably as part of the pared-down trio (with John and Ringo) that gave Lennon's *John Lennon/Plastic Ono Band* album its bracingly spare, primitive sound (though Yoko Ono is also credited on the sleeve, rather unfortunately, for contributing "wind"). Moving to Los Angeles in the 1970s, Voormann cut a Zelig-like swath through rock-royalty circles, sessioning for, among others, HARRY NILSSON, Randy Newman, Carly Simon, and Gary "Dream Weaver" Wright.

Vox AC-30. Handsome but puny British-manufactured amplifier-speaker that first gained attention during the Beatles' early, scream-drenched appearances in America. Cheap and eminently portable, the AC-30 became standard issue among the hordes of American garage bands that arose in the British Invasion's wake. (The amp is recognizable on old *Shindig* episodes by the crisscross gilt pattern on its woven brown speaker cloth.) Among the purists who maintain fealty to the modest, tube-generated sound of the AC-30 is, surprisingly, guitarist Brian May of the bombast purveyors Queen. *My* AC-30 *is old and battered, but you just can't beat that warm, intimate sound.*

FIFTH BEATLES, IN ORDER OF WORTHINESS

1. Brian Epstein, *group's manager until his death in 1967*

2. George Martin, *producer and arranger on most of the group's recorded output*

3. Stu Sutcliffe, *bassist, actual fifth Beatle in the band's short-lived, Hamburg-era five-man lineup*

4. Billy Preston, *keyboardist, sat in with Beatles on fractious* Let It Be *sessions; later became a contender for "Sixth Rolling Stone"*

5. Klaus Voormann, *chum of band since Hamburg days, designed* Revolver *and* Anthology *covers, played bass on solo albums by John, George, and Ringo*

6. Mal Evans, *eternally loyal roadie*

7. Neil Aspinall, *eternally loyal tour manager, later appointed head of Apple Corps, Ltd.*

8. Derek Taylor, *press officer, ghostwriter of Epstein's memoir* A Cellarful of Noise

9. Maharishi Mahesh Yogi, *spiritual adviser, hosted the group in Rishikesh in 1968*

10. Eric Clapton, *guest-soloed on "While My Guitar Gently Weeps"*

11. Murray "the K" Kaufman, *WINS DJ during the Beatles' first U.S. visit and inventor of the term "Fifth Beatle" (in dubious reference to himself)*

Occasionally Cited, but Unworthy of Fifth Beatle Consideration

Pete Best (drummer sacked in favor of Ringo before the band's recording career began in earnest), Andy White (EMI session drummer brought in to play on "Love Me Do" and "P.S. I Love You"), and Jimmy Nicol (replacement drummer for the band's 1964 tour of Australia, during which Ringo was ill)

Wachtel, Waddy. Ubiquitous, visually amusing session guitarist, immediately recognizable for his bony build, long, frizzy, center-parted strawberry-blond hair, and circular wire-rim glasses. Having risen through the L.A. studio ranks as an associate of Warren Zevon's, Wachtel served as a de facto fifth member of THE SECTION in the seventies, lending his riffage to Zevon's, James Taylor's, and Linda Ronstadt's records. He has since carved out a lucrative career as a hired gun, accepting studio and touring commissions from, among others, Stevie Nicks, Keith Richards, and stealth Rock Snob Adam Sandler.

Wagoner, Porter. Long-serving OLD-SCHOOL country star enjoying new cred as an ALT.COUNTRY godfather and as the re-ROOTSified Dolly Parton's original springboard to fame. An affably cornball, rhinestone-studded Opry favorite, Wagoner brought Parton aboard his syndicated TV show in 1967 as a singing partner. Though it was Parton who went on to be the huge crossover COUNTRYPOLITAN star after their split in 1974, Wagoner's out-of-print concept albums and excursions into country-PSYCH (most notably with the bizarre 1972 song "Rubber Room") have brought him a new hipster following, even as he continues to ply his trade before mulleted Nashville audiences.

Porter Wagoner

Walker, Scott. Morose crooner, born Noel Scott Engel in Ohio, who first achieved success as part of the Walker Brothers, a sixties teenybop trio (not actually brothers) that scored a hit with BURT BACHARACH and Hal David's "Make It Easy on Yourself." Walker's lasting Rock Snob appeal comes from the string of eponymous solo albums he made in the late sixties and early seventies, which are worshipped in his adopted homeland of Great Britain. Setting his ridiculously vibrato'd, Vegas-worthy wail against Kurt Weill–esque orchestral arrangements, he became the dark knight of schlock. In 1995, Walker briefly resurfaced with an impenetrable, Trent Reznor–influenced comeback album entitled *Tilt.*

Webb, Jimmy. Oklahoma-born, Los Angeles–based songwriter who has enjoyed a BURT BACHARACH–like renaissance after years in too-soft-for-these-times exile. The author of such sixties cocktail-pop classics as "MacArthur Park" and "Up, Up and Away," Webb has performed occasional cabaret dates in recent years, sometimes in the company of Glen Campbell, who scored Top 10 hits with Webb's "Wichita Lineman" and "By the Time I Get to Phoenix."

White label. Industry term for an advance promotional copy of a new song, so named for the unadorned white labels slapped on early pressings of twelve-inch vinyl singles. White labels are the bread and butter of newness-obsessed club DJs, whose worst nightmare is to appear three seconds behind the times. *Right, after we finish snorting this Charlie, let's go down the club, mate; my mate Gavin is DJing and he's got a stack of* white labels *fresh in from New York.*

Whitfield, Norman. The Snobworthiest of Motown's producer-composers, favored over the Holland/Dozier/Holland team and label founder Berry Gordy because of his ambitious arrangements and his genre-straddling excursions into PSYCH-soul. Whitfield led the Temptations away from their "My Girl" tranquility and into the rougher, weirder waters of "Ball of Confusion," "Papa Was a Rolling Stone," and "I Can't Get Next to You." Having also written and produced Edwin Starr's "War" and Marvin Gaye's "I Heard It Through the Grapevine," Whitfield wins Snob plaudits for having boldly confronted the reality that the sync-dancing, shimmying days of early Motown wouldn't cut it in the cynical climate of the Nixonian era.

Whodini. Unreconstructedly OLD-SCHOOL Brooklyn rap trio who have risen in Snob esteem by virtue of not getting the same due as contemporaries Run-DMC. Less skeletal than most early-eighties hip-hop, Whodini's hits—among them "Friends," "One Love," and "Freaks Come Out at Night"—had more R&B underpinning to them, anticipating New Jack Swing, and, in the bolero-hatted John "Ecstacy" Fletcher, the group had hip-hop's first sex symbol. *Yo, I was down with* Whodini *when Eminem was in his trailer watching* Sesame Street*!*

Wilco. Former ALT.COUNTRY standard-bearers whose ventures into eclectic pop have earned them the designation of America's premier crit-rock band, with hangdog frontman Jeff Tweedy now as untouchable as RICHARD THOMPSON. Wilco's 2001 album, *Yankee Hotel Foxtrot*, became a Snob cause célèbre when the band's label, Reprise, deemed it unreleasable, impelling Tweedy to make the new songs available on the band's own Web site. The rapturous Snob response induced another label, Nonesuch, to purchase and release *Yankee Hotel Foxtrot*—a Snob-stoking triumph against "the Man," since Nonesuch and Reprise's common corporate parent, AOL Time

Warner, effectively paid for the album twice. *Somewhere in heaven, John Lennon, Gram Parsons, and Lowell George are jamming, and I bet it sounds just like* Wilco.

Willner, Hal. Genial, well-connected producer who presided over the boomer good-taste epidemic of the eighties, working as both the musical director of *Saturday Night Live* and the mastermind of a series of Snob-worthy tribute albums that shrewdly captured the burgeoning "Honey, let's wear retro-fifties eyeglasses and embrace pre-rock idioms" ethos of the era. His first tribute album, from 1981, featured the likes of Deborah Harry, BILL FRISELL, and Wynton Marsalis paying homage to Italian soundtrack composer NINO ROTA. Subsequent Willner projects have featured such Snob blue-chippers as John Zorn, Tom Waits, Elvis Costello, SUN RA, and Lou Reed commemorating the disparate yet exquisitely cherry-picked oeuvres of Thelonius Monk, Charles Mingus, Kurt Weill, Edgar Allan Poe, TIM BUCKLEY, and Walt Disney.

Wilson, Brian. Mentally fragile Beach Boys leader. While revered by normal people for the catchiness and ingenuity of such hits as "I Get Around" and "California Girls," Wilson is revered by Rock Snobs more for his sensitive orchestral-pop masterwork, *Pet Sounds*; for the ambition and general way-outness of its abandoned follow-up, *Smile*, the unraveling of which sealed his reputation as a misunderstood genius forever persecuted by his own demons and "the Man"; and even for

Brian Wilson

his fragmentary output from the seventies and eighties, which offers only evanescent moments of his sixties-standard brilliance. Still a palpably haunted figure, Wilson has been well enough in recent years to mount live-concert versions of *Pet Sounds* and *Smile* (the latter of which he recorded in 2004), though furious Snob debate rages over whether these efforts are evidence of his still-burning genius or the too-generously received work of a barely participatory man whose proficient backing musicians compensate for his tentativeness.

Wilson, Dennis. Strikingly handsome middle brother of the Beach Boy Wilsons. Long suspected of being a marginally talented surfer-stoner dude who was merely along for the ride with genius older brother BRIAN WILSON and golden-voiced kid brother Carl—though nominally the group's drummer, he often ceded his sticks to WRECKING CREW stalwart Hal Blaine—Dennis surprised fans when, as a novice songwriter in the late sixties, he ably crafted emotionally fraught ballads; his out-of-print 1977 solo album, *Pacific Ocean Blue*, is a major cause célèbre among Snobs. An even more tragic figure than mentally ill sibling Brian, Dennis befriended Charles Manson, facilitating the killer's entrée into the sixties L.A.-rock artistocracy. Dennis died in 1983 in penurious, booze-addled circumstances, ironically by drowning in the Beach Boys' beloved Pacific. The title of a 2001 Dennis biography, *The Real Beach Boy*, neatly encapsulates the fervent ethos of Dennis Snobs.

Wilson, Robert. Inscrutable Texas-born stage director who has made a career of cooking up difficult but rewarding quasi-operas and musical happenings, usually at the Brooklyn Academy of Music or in some German city where people go for that sort of thing. Having made his name in 1976 with his Philip Glass collaboration *Einstein on the Beach*, a four-and-a-half-hour opus that celebrated the physicist's work with recourse to neither character nor plot, Wilson has since charged through contemporary music's obtuse-artperson firmament, working with Tom Waits, Lou Reed, David Byrne, and Laurie Anderson on theatrical projects of epic scale, visual and sonic audacity, and often punitive length.

Wilson, Tom. Harvard-educated African-American record producer who, though his personal taste ran to jazz, built up the world's most impeccable rock-production credentials in the mid-sixties, not only guiding Bob Dylan through the "going electric" process on *Bringing It All Back Home*, but also producing albums by Simon and Garfunkel, the Velvet Underground, NICO, and Frank Zappa. Wilson's relationship with Dylan began in 1963, when Columbia Records roped him into completing the sessions for *The Freewheelin' Bob Dylan* after Dylan's rapacious manager, Albert Grossman, had had a falling out with JOHN HAMMOND. On the heels of his short but crucial collaboration with ZIMMY (it was Wilson who enlisted Al Kooper, his buddy, to play the famous organ part on "Like a Rolling Stone"), Wilson helped Simon and Garfunkel transition out of acoustic-folkie obsolescence and became the East Coast A&R director of the Verve label, signing the Velvets and Mothers, honing his legendary ladykilling skills, and generally exuding an air of skinny-lapeled, John Cassavetes–movie cool.

TEN 'LOST MASTERPIECES'

There is no greater rallying cry for Rock Snobs than the "lost masterpiece," the album done in by public indifference, record-company mismanagement, or its author's own eccentricities and travails. Herewith, some of the most Snob-celebrated specimens of the genre.

Purported masterpiece: *Smile*, by the Beach Boys, 1967

'Lost' because: Brian Wilson suffered a mental breakdown while recording it; the project was shelved and left incomplete until the Snob gestalt persuaded Wilson to give it another go in 2004.

Purported masterpiece: *The Kinks Are the Village Green Preservation Society*, by the Kinks, 1968

'Lost' because: It came out a touch too late to capitalize on the 1967 vogue for pastoral Victorian whimsy, instead getting trampled underfoot by the new wave of loud, bluesy power trios. Though it actually *was* the best album of 1968.

Purported masterpiece: *Odessa*, by the Bee Gees, 1969

'Lost' because: No one wanted to hear a has-been Swinging London boy band attempt a conceptual, orchestral song suite; a disco comeback would prove a better idea. Barry Gibb remains genuinely puzzled by Snob adoration of this album.

Purported masterpiece: *Oar*, by Skip Spence, 1969

'Lost' because: There wasn't exactly a ready audience for this sparse, spooky snapshot of an acid casualty's brain, recorded on the fly shortly after Spence—formerly of the Jefferson Airplane and Moby Grape—had been released from the psychiatric ward of a prison. By 1999, however, *Oar* had birthed an all-star quasi-sequel, *More Oar*, on which such eccentric but eminently sane artists as Beck, Tom Waits, and Robert Plant paid respectful tribute.

Purported masterpiece: *Genuine Imitation Life Gazette*, by the Four Seasons, 1969

'Lost' because: No one wanted to hear the affable New Jersey *paisanos* go all baroque and concepty—

no one, that is, except revisionist twenty-first-century Snobs.

Purported masterpiece: The original version of *Blood on the Tracks*, by Bob Dylan, 1974

'Lost' because: Dylan decided he didn't like the ultra-low-key treatment of his marital-strife diary and rerecorded the album almost in its entirety, with the new results issued early in 1975. Many, if not most, shut-in Dylan Snobs prefer bootlegs of the first version to the official release.

Purported masterpiece: *Born to Be With You*, by Dion, 1975

'Lost' because: The ex-"Wanderer" was a commercial pariah by the mid-seventies, and the album's similarly unfashionable producer, Phil Spector, willed that the album only be released in the U.K. The album's 2001 rerelease won major plaudits, even though its sodden, shag-carpeted production will sound anachronistic for decades to come.

Purported masterpiece: *Pacific Ocean Blue*, by Dennis Wilson, 1977

'Lost' because: The die had been cast, and the Beach Boys were now a backward-looking nostalgia act, meaning that neither public adoration nor record-company support would be forthcoming for the hardest-living Wilson brother's surprisingly soulful set of songs.

Purported masterpiece: *The Black Album*, by Prince, 1987

'Lost' because: Prince shelved it after deciding, allegedly on religious grounds, that it was too raunchy for mainstream release. More likely, he probably felt that letting it slip out as a bootleg was a canny career move—especially given that the "clean" album with which it was officially replaced was called *Lovesexy* and featured him nude on the cover.

Purported masterpiece: *Spirit of Eden*, by Talk Talk, 1988

'Lost' because: No one cared about a repentant haircut band's quest for organic, anti-synth gravitas.

Wire. Gaunt Anglo-punks whose jerky 1977 debut, *Pink Flag*, crammed twenty-two ascetic tunes into less than forty minutes and cemented the word "angular" in the rock-crit lexicon. The expanded vision and musicality of Wire's two subsequent albums made the band a cred-building name-drop for the decades to come. (The second-tier Britpop band Elastica was so Wire-influenced that it was legally required to hand over songwriting royalties.) True to the punk ethic, Wire disbanded in 1980, declaring itself artistically mined out, but broke the mystique by reforming six years later for an extended and inauspicious second fling.

Wondermints, the. Nerdy, POWER-POP–loving cult band more readily embraced in cutesy-pop–mad Japan than in its native Los Angeles. Despite their relatively low domestic profile, the Wondermints have twice hit the dork-fantasist mother lode, first when Mike Myers tapped them to perform the theme song for the original *Austin Powers* movie, and then when BRIAN WILSON asked them to be his backing band when he toured live versions of his *Pet Sounds* and *Smile* albums.

Wrecking Crew. Crack team of sixties-era Los Angeles session musicians whose number included drummer Hal Blaine, bassists Carol Kaye and Ray Pohlman, keyboardists Larry Knechtel and Leon Russell, saxophonist Steve Douglas, and guitarists Jerry Cole and Tommy Tedesco. Often summoned at odd hours to execute the tricky, ambitious arrangements of Phil Spector, BRIAN WILSON, and JACK NITZSCHE.

Wyatt, Robert. Former drummer and singer of THE SOFT MACHINE, who, after a 1973 accident that left him a paraplegic, grew a long beard, took up Marxist politics, and began a solo career that has had Snobs writhing in ecstasy ever since. Singing in a fragile, keening tenor that the Japanese electro-composer Ryuichi Sakamoto has famously described as "the saddest voice in the world," Wyatt has typically set his poetic, witty plaints against stark, keyboard-dominated settings, most notably on *Rock Bottom*, the album he recorded less than a year after his accident, and on his 1982 version of Elvis Costello's "Shipbuilding," which questioned the Thatcherist right's jingoism during the Falkland Islands War.

Robert Wyatt

XTC. Acutely English pop group that initially, in the mid-seventies, tried to position itself as a spiky new wave outfit (original name: Helium Kidz), but gradually revealed itself to be an exurban, nerdy version of the Beatles, with principal songwriter Andy Partridge playing a combined Lennon-McCartney to secondary songwriter Colin Moulding's George Harrison. Studio-bound since 1982, when the band quit touring because of Partridge's stage fright, XTC's intricately melodic songs—too pastoral and proficient to be called POWER-POP—have won them a small but dedicated band of American-Anglophile followers who delight in Partridge's references to "wire toasting forks" and "potting sheds." Not without senses of humor about their retro leanings and hyper-Albionic sensibility, Partridge, Moulding et al. have also recorded two psychedelic parody albums under the pseudonym the Dukes of Stratosphear.

Yé-yé girls. Swinging-sixties French ingenues who applied their inherent Franco-opacity and Euro-cheesiness to the fluffy girl-pop styles then in vogue in Britain and America, alchemically achieving a highly sexualized result. The most famous yé-yé girls were Brigitte Bardot (wearing her singer's hat), FRANÇOISE HARDY, and France Gall, but hardcore enthusiasts revel in delving deeper, obsessing over such forgotten single-named stars as Hédika, Géraldine, Sophie, and French national treasure Sheila (née Annie Chancel), renowned for her pre-Britney schoolgirl outfits and her yé-yé anthem "L'École Est Fini" (School Is Over!).

Zimmy. Insiderist nickname for Bob Dylan, favored by shut-in Dylanologists in their painstaking discussions of their godhead's oeuvre; derived from Dylan's actual surname, Zimmerman. *Man,* Blood on the Tracks *is just a harrowing document of* Zimmy'*s divorce.*

Zombies, the. Melodic mid-sixties English pop band whose civilian status as a three-hit wonder ("She's Not There," "Tell Her No," "Time of the Season") is overridden in Snob circles by its authorship of the 1967 PSYCH-pop masterwork *Odessey and Oracle* (so misspelled because the cover artist messed up). Recorded with no concessions to the marketplace, since the band members knew they were going to split up upon the album's completion, *Odessey and Oracle* edges out the oppressively familiar *Sgt. Pepper's Lonely Hearts Club Band* as the Snob's preferred distillation of summer-of-love utopianism and floral-pop ingenuity.

Zoso. Preferred Snob nickname for Led Zeppelin's untitled fourth album, also known as *Led Zeppelin IV, Four*

Symbols, Old Codger with Bundle of Sticks on His Back, and *The One with "Stairway" on It.* Derived from the quasi-runic symbol Jimmy Page chose to represent himself on the back cover, which, though it's alleged to have a sinister, secret meaning, has nevertheless been appropriated as the name of a Led Zep tribute band in California. *Dude, I would kill to get the kick-drum sound that Bonzo had on* Zoso.

Zoso

Rock Snob Visual Quiz!

How good a spotter of Snob-certified people and things are you? Test your Snob knowledge by matching the figures on the left with their descriptions on the right!

1. 

A. Doomed, sensual Beach Boy Dennis Wilson

2. 

B. New Age pioneer Terry Riley

3. 

C. Creation Records overlord Alan McGee

4. 

D. Inveterate session pro Jeff "Skunk" Baxter

5. 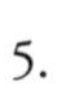  E. "Rock Family Tree" inventor Pete Frame

6.  F. The DJ-indispensable Technics SL-1200 turntable

7.  G. Junk-shop composer-inventor Harry Partch

8.  H. Ill-starred glamsters the New York Dolls

9.  I. Orch-pop forgotten man David Axelrod

Answers: 1. B; 2. I; 3. F; 4. A; 5. C; 6. H; 7. D; 8. G; 9. E.

About the Authors

© Nina Bramhall

David Kamp, a lifelong music snob, has been a writer and editor for *Vanity Fair* and *GQ* for over a decade and began his career at *Spy* magazine, the satirical monthly. He lives in New York.

© Shawn Mortensen

Steven Daly has been a music and arts journalist since 1987, contributing to *The Face, Spin, Interview, GQ,* and *Details*. In 1994, Daly cowrote *alt.culture*, an exhaustive reference book on global youth culture that was widely praised in the United States and abroad. He became a contributing editor at *Rolling Stone* in 1998 and joined *Vanity Fair* the following year in the same capacity. Daly lives in New York.

About the Illustrator

Ross MacDonald's illustrations have appeared in many magazines from *The New Yorker* and *Vanity Fair* to *Rolling Stone* and the *Wall Street Journal.* His first children's book, *Another Perfect Day*, won *Publishers Weekly*'s Best Book of the Year for its category. MacDonald lives in Connecticut with his wife, two children, four cats, and a large collection of nineteenth-century type and printing equipment.